Design Sources for the Fiber Artist

Design Sources for the Fiber Artist

Irene Waller

Davis Publications, Inc.
Worcester, Massachusetts

Printed in the United States of America
Library of Congress Catalog Card Number: 78-51290
ISBN: 0-87192-098-0

Printing: Davis Press, Inc.
Binding: A. Horowitz & Son
Type: Korinna Regular and Bold
Graphic Design: South Bay Graphics

Consulting Editors: George F. Horn and Sarita R. Rainey

10 9 8 7 6 5 4 3 2 1

Contents

Introduction

This book is about a way of seeing and of selecting images from our environment. We are surrounded by a visual world which is a never-ceasing and ever-changing source of stimulation. We need only explore it to expand our visual awareness, from which we can develop fresh concepts and techniques. This book will not only inspire new creative ideas but will offer direct, practical help for designers who work with fiber, yarn and fabric.

Part 1

About Design

Design Sources

The stimuli which spur artists on to creative efforts are many. These stimuli often act as irritants — causing artists to be dissatisfied until their original idea or sensation has been transformed into a product that reveals their inner vision. Many matters stimulate visual imagery: abstract ideas, interactions with the environment, the materials we use, or even the techniques we adopt to actualize our ideas. We will examine some of these sources more closely in relation to the work of some contemporary fiber artists.

Abstract Ideas

The first source is that of totally abstract ideas, i.e., mental concepts or speculations, which can be given substance in visual form. For example, Jindřich Vohánka, a Czechoslovakian artist, expresses his concern with philosophy and man's relationship with God in his flat shaped tapestries (Figure 1). Polish artist Magdalena Abakanowicz reveals her preoccupation with the speed at which technology is overtaking humans in her art. Her textile sculptures in rough basic materials, such as jute, provoke us to think about ourselves and our environment beyond the limits of natural laws (Figure 2). Inge Vahle, a West German artist, is also concerned with the menace of technology. She transmits this message in vast machine-like impersonal and aggressive black sisal shapes (Figures 3 & 4).

These works reveal the artists' attitudes to either timeless or current issues. They identify the artist as the messenger, the prophet and, in our age, the cautioner. The works spotlight the situation in which we find ourselves in a time of cosmic stress and uncertainty.

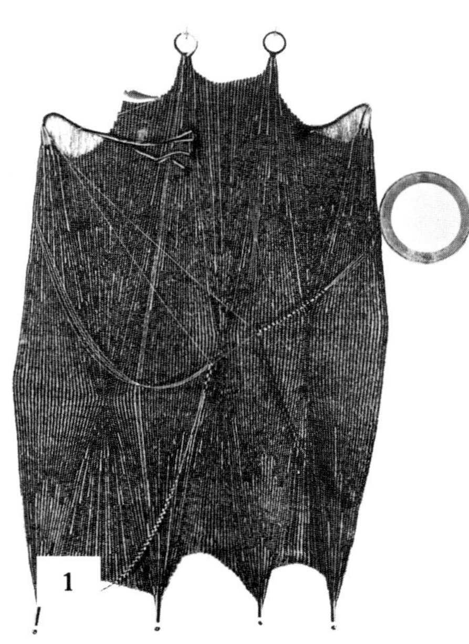

1. **La Visite D'Aldebaran** by Jindřich Vohánka. 10'2" x 6'4".

2. **Altérations** (1975) by Magdalena Abakanowicz. 29'6" x 4'5" x 2'4½". Moulded jute fabric, fiber, and yarn.

3

4

3. **Induktionfield** (1971) by Inge Vahle. 12' x 8'9" x 1'3". Black sisal winding and knotting. Photo by P. Heilmann.

4D. Detail of **Induktionfield.** Photo by P. Heilmann.

5. **Variabil Noir** (1975) by Jagoda Buic. 12' x 20' x 3'4". Woven and bound three-dimensional forms.

6D. Detail of **Variabil Noir.**

7
8

The Environment

Both the natural and industrial worlds can elicit various reactions from us. The artificial world of skyscrapers, traffic, and lights can appear menacing in one instant and rich in design the next. The natural world can overwhelm us with its storms and cataclysms or astonish us with its inexhaustible richness and organic beauty. In this field it is Jagoda Buic, the Yugoslav artist, who is without peer. Her portrayals in dyed sisal of subjects like rocks, cliffs, and fortresses take us into the heart of the matter. Standing before a piece of her monumental work one feels a debt to the artist for enlightening and enriching us and for conferring upon us a more intense and absolute knowledge of what rocks, stones, and fortresses are about (Figures 5 & 6).

Textile Materials

For many artists, the handling of materials not only incites their desire to create but influences the form they give to their materials. Sculptor Henry Moore, for example, uses stone to depict his conception of the relationship of humans to their environment. His sculptures are massive and his human forms are rendered with a classic yet primitive simplicity. The viewer inescapably wonders if Moore has allowed the qualities of the stone - its smoothness, roughness, and weight - to influence the forms of his figures. It would seem reasonable to suppose that much can evolve from the interaction of an idea with the materials chosen to fulfill that idea.

In the world of textile art, we find that artists are highly influenced by their materials. Sheila Hicks' work seems to spring from the innate qualities of the silks, linens, and wools she uses. In her winding and wrapping techniques, she displays the soft luster and glowing colors of silk and wool with sensuous mastery (Figure 7). She also reveals her sensivity to linen by emphasizing its crisp, clear-cut characteristics (Figure 8).

Textile Techniques

Techniques often shape the direction of an artist's work. Like materials, techniques have unique properties that can become an important vehicle for expressing an artist's intentions. Peter Collingwood's techniques for creating linear and angular patterns admirably convey his feeling for line and order. He moves blocks of warp from one placing to another in the loom and on this angular, rather than vertical warp, weaves sparsely with linen and steel rod (Figure 9).

However, great art defies categories. The above is not meant to state that Hicks' work is only about materials, Buic's work only about the natural world, Abakanowicz's work only about abstract concepts and Collingwood's only about a technique. Each contains elements, in varying proportions, of all. Defining the categories is merely a mechanism by which to indicate the varied nature of the bases of artists' creative urges and thus attempting to define a total field, while stating that this book is concerned with the second category — the visual stimuli which are all around us.

7. Bas-Relief in linen and gold threads (1976) by Sheila Hicks.

8D. Detail of Bas-Relief.

9. **Macrogauze** by Peter Collingwood. Linen and steel rod.

10. **Zanzibar** (1972) by Barbara Chase-Riboud. 9'6" x 2'10" x 10". Polished bronze and synthetic silk.

Visual Stimuli
from the Environment — and the Creative Process

The book's contents were compiled with a two-fold purpose. First and most importantly, to put before the reader a copious collection of stimulating visual images; images owing their quality to nothing and no one but their own factual existence — they are **there.** Stimuli are all around us even in the most unpromising circumstances — rain on the window, smoke billowing from chimneys, particles of dust in the air, and sunlight patterns across the floor.

Sadly, we grow visually lazy; we can switch off our eyes as we can switch off our ears and others of our senses. If we close our ears it may be quite deliberate, the shutting out of extraneous noise in order to concentrate on thought, but even when hearing pleasing sounds, we can still shut them out. You may have experienced this while attending a concert. For a while you heard nothing in a real sense, so preoccupied were you with the clatter of your thoughts that you did not relax and allow the music your total attention. We, even those of us whose very central concern is with the visual, can do the same thing with our eyes. I suggest that we take another look, that we reeducate our eyes, that we learn to look as if we were seeing for the first time, as do the young, or to look with the eyes of a stranger to this particular earth. The result is constant visual pleasure and absorption.

The second purpose of the book was to suggest some of the ways in which these stimuli can be translated into textile terms — textile in the broadest sense, using a wide variety of techniques. The design sources are mine, therefore the work illustrated had, of necessity, to be mine. In an endeavor to be general rather than too personal, often parts rather than entire pieces of work are illustrated. For the same reason, the illustrations of textile works were purposely kept smaller than the illustrations of the design sources.

Many images are recorded in the mind and combined together to create numerous outcomes. It is, then, important that the design sources in the main section of the book are taken, not as a series of isolated subjects, but very much as a whole. Sometimes the link between what we see and create is direct. The creation of a wall hanging may well be the direct outcome of flying over snow-covered areas (Pages 36, 37). More often, the links are tenuous and complex. What we see is not necessarily what we create. An image may trigger off unexpected ideas or may act merely as a catalyst to unify other images and thoughts. An artist may combine several visual impressions into a personal whole which does not mirror the actual world. One single piece of work may contain tiny traces of many varied visual stimuli.

Recording Source Material

In order to become familiar with our subjects, we generally find that we must record them. Drawing and photography are two important means of discovering and recording what we see. These records often provide the groundwork for transforming our initial ideas into completed artistic statements.

Drawing

Drawing is one way of identifying a subject and is integral to an artist's development. The act of drawing involves and unites the observer with his subject.

Drawing, unfortunately, often has an air of mystery associated with it. The first stage of drawing is to learn to relax about it. The second is to constantly have a notebook at hand, a small purse - or pocket-sized pad, and draw whenever there is a spare moment. Fluidity and ease will come with practice. You may draw a whole scene or just fragments of it — for example, the fold of a garment or tablecloth or the shape of a shadow in a doorway. Your drawings may range from accurate and literal observations of natural forms to abstract impressions. The drawings of Afro-American sculptress, Barbara Chase-Riboud are midway between these two tendencies (Figures 11).

It is of utmost importance, especially for the beginner, to **look** at the subject. Observe, draw **what is there**; not necessarily with the shorthand of outline but in terms of tone and mass.

Media other than pencil and charcoal, such as paint, mixed media, pastels, and inks, can all be used to record impressions. Sax Shaw, a tapestry artist from Scotland, makes water color notes for a tapestry while "thinking in wool."

Photography

The camera is an invaluable piece of equipment for recording source material. All of the source material presented in Part 2 of this book has been recorded with a camera. For this particular purpose, the camera had a unique and indispensible quality — a certain anonymity and impartiality. When we draw it involves a personal act; we begin to translate parts of, or the entire, object into our own personal interpretations. When we use the camera, no such thing **need** happen. The subject of the photograph **can** be recorded exactly as it appears. The resulting image is as useful to others as it is to the photographer as no personal interpretation has taken place in either the taking of the photograph or in the printing of it. However, it should be noted that the photographic image — like any other artistic media — can be highly expressive in the hands of an experienced artist/photographer.

Many factors must be considered to obtain clear images with the camera.

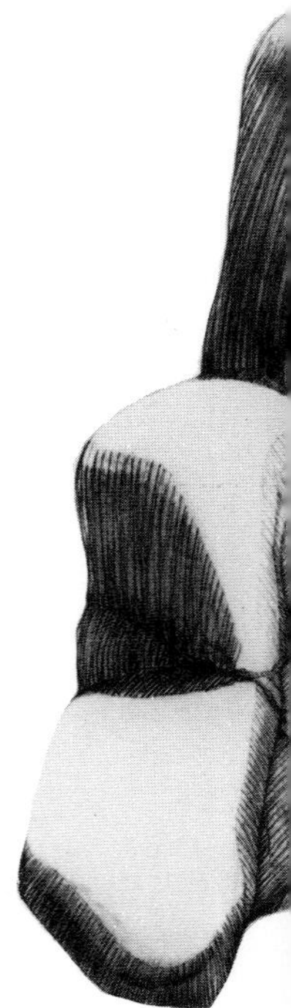

11

11

A camera should be technically well made and have a fine lens capable of close work. A good light meter, whether separate or built-in, is essential. A good quality close-range lens with extension rings to bring distant subjects closer will give extra dimension to the results.

Black and white prints and color transparencies meet most artists' needs. Color prints are not recommended as they are costly and often misrepresent colors. Some artists carry two cameras, one loaded with black and white film, the other with film for transparencies. To reduce the bulk, it is a good idea to carry a lens that will fit both cameras. Different results are achieved with these two types of film. Black and white prints delineate shadow, line, shape, texture and give instant viewing while transparencies provide accurate color and are good for group showing. The subject we wish to photograph often makes its own demands. Figure 16 in Design Sources, for instance, could only have been taken in color while Figure 137 demanded black and white treatment.

It is important to use the camera effectively. When taking pictures it is vital to define exactly what we want to capture. If the texture of a eucalyptus bark intrigues us as a subject we will learn more about its character by photographing just one section of it than the whole tree (Figure 22). In turn, a close-up of some waves may tell us more about their movement than a long shot of an entire body of water. It is easy to include irrelevancies in our records of objects. Learning to be selective is of utmost importance and will greatly aid our design efforts.

It is often useful to have film printed as a contact sheet. By studying the images with a magnifying glass, we can determine which photographs are of superior quality and have them made into prints. These prints can be pinned around the work area so that we may study them closely and gently absorb their impact.

11. Two drawings by Barbara Chase-Riboud.

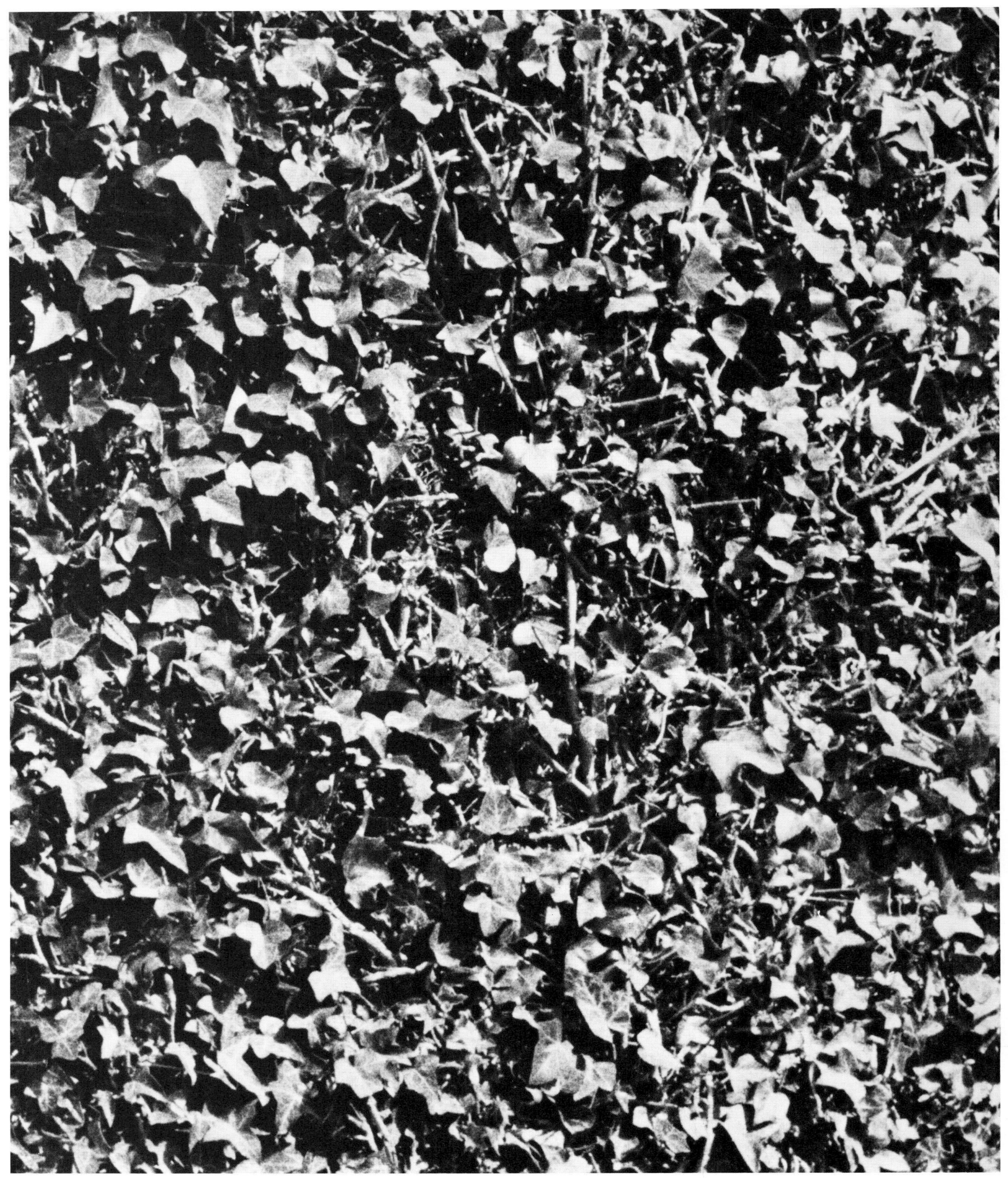

Conclusion

The message of this book is **look** and **absorb.** As Geoffrey Fletcher states in his **Elements of Sketching,** "Reality and experience are lying around — take what you need." By experiencing and exploring our environment, we learn and grow. The more we look, the more we will nurture and develop our visual awareness.

Part 2

Design Sources and Textile Objects

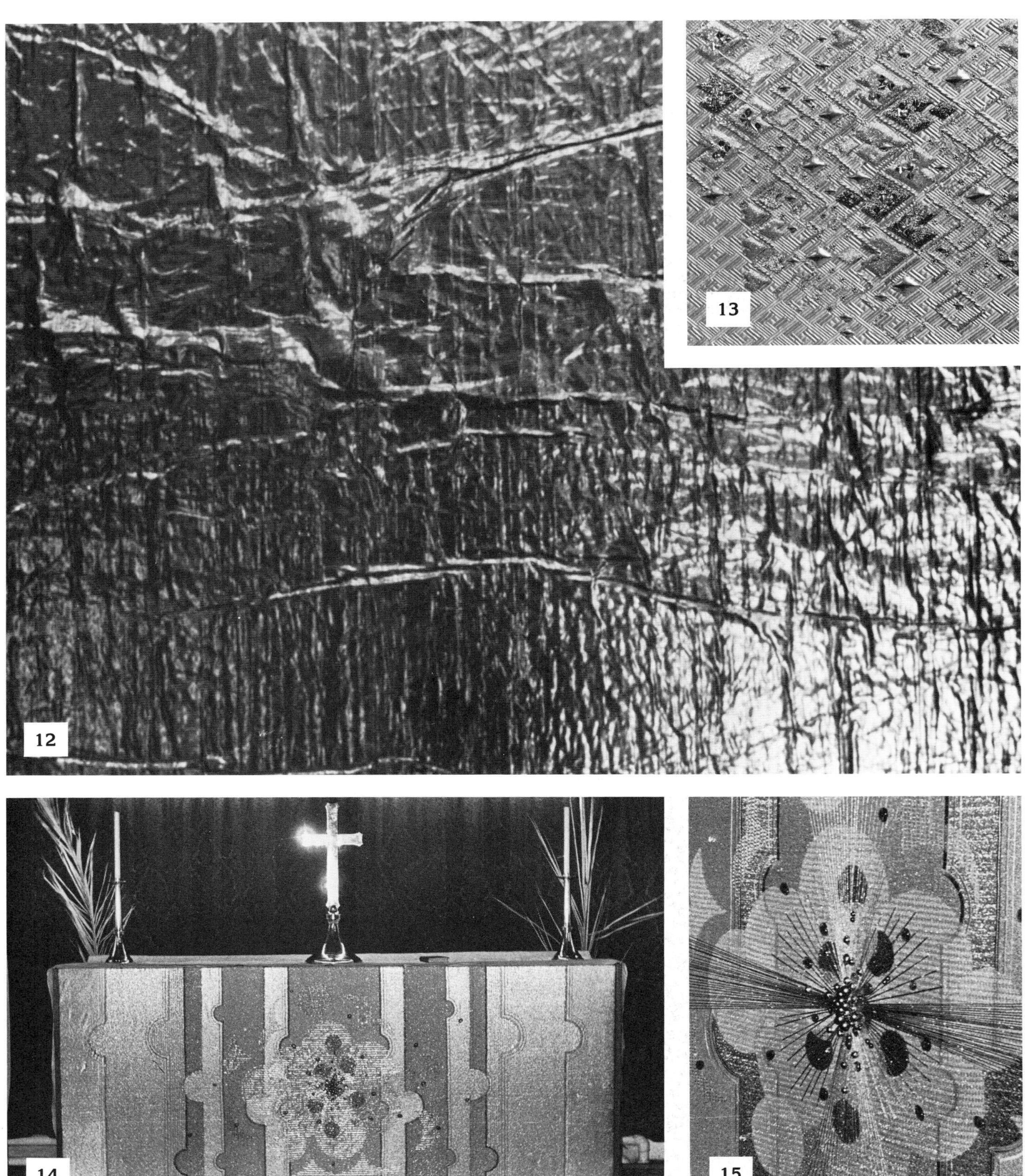
12
13
14
15

Metallic Surfaces

12. Aluminum foil is used to insulate the outside of a walk-in refrigerator. Its sheen and reflective properties enchance its irregularities and create a striking study of silvers.

13. Embroidered silver panel. Silver is explored in many different materials — Jacquard fabric, velvet, smooth fabrics, beads, braids, nets, and leather. The technique is padded appliqué.

14. Altar frontal. Flat appliqué, embellished with machine-embroidery, beads, and stretched gold threads.

15D. Detail of altar frontal.

16. This battered tuba presents a variety of shapes, textures, and an incredible range of golds.

18

19

17

Trees

Trees, among the many natural forms, offer a wide range of visual possibilities, from the bark of an individual tree to a deep grove, in summer or winter, alone or as part of a landscape.

Tree Bark

17. This close-up of birch bark was taken late in the day in a very golden light. The gold ranges from almost orange-brown to green. Interest arises not only from the interplay of textured and smooth surfaces but also from the repetitive shapes of different size in the textured area. This bark partly inspired two textile designs.

18. Like the birch bark, this altar frontal features a broad range of golds. Its ground is hand-woven and its overlaying motif-shapes are attached by appliqué. In this technique, the ground weave consists of two warps — one is close-set and substantial to produce whatever ground cloth is desired; the other has very fine strong threads, set one end to every half inch and is entered on one or two separate harnesses. The weave can use as few as three harnesses. When the fine threads are lifted, very bulky slubs of weft, such as unspun wool, velvet, fur fabric, braids or beads can be inserted at random. The fine threads then disappear below the surface or into the weave of the cloth until they are required again. They hold the bulky wefts firmly and invisibly. Because this method of holding is unobtrusive, fabrics of great textural surface interest can be created.

19D. Detail of altar frontal. The appliqué crosses are of padded velvet and are embellished with braids and paste jewels.

20. This mural, created for a newspaper office, was woven by the same technique as the altar frontal. Woven in icy blues and silvers, the nebulous shapes are the actual type used in the newspaper printing process and the scrap metal which comes from the typemaking machinery. The metal shapes were first held by fabric adhesive and then stitched over with "invisible" nylon dressmaker's thread. Several applications of polyurethane clear varnish protect the metal from tarnish.

21D. Detail of office mural.

22. Eucalyptus bark is distinctive for its vertical twisting, intertwining, and contrast of textures. Each segment of it offers rich possibilities for design.

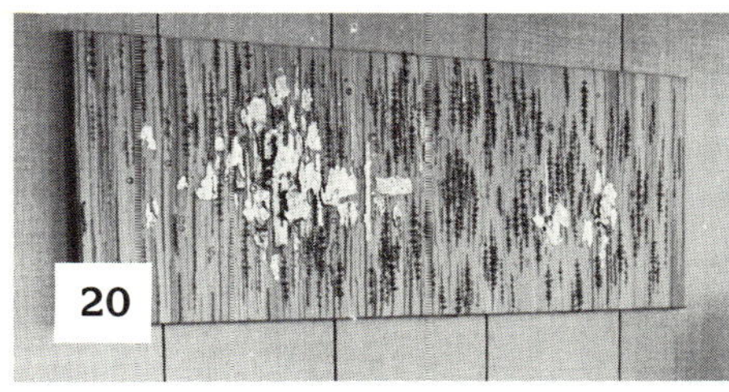
20

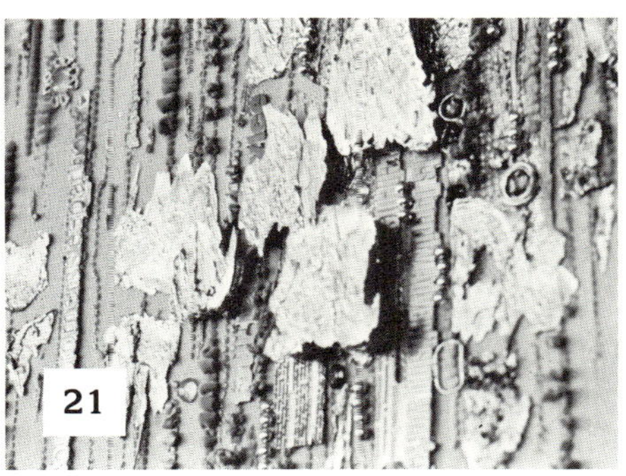
21

22

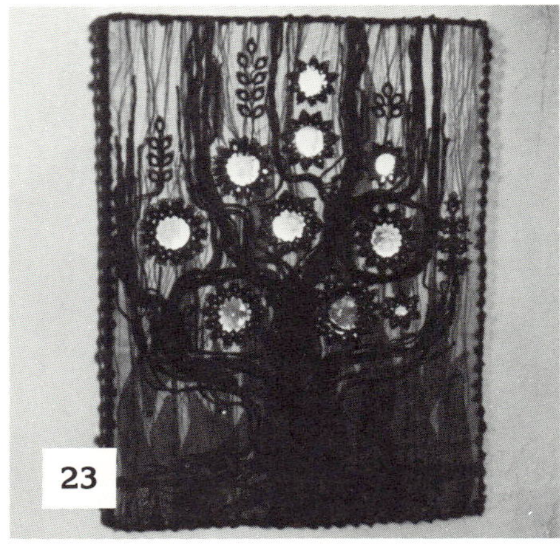

23. Collage, part of which was influenced by the eucalyptus bark. The materials used are carpet wools, braids, mirrors, and beads on a fabric, net and thread ground.

24D. Detail of collage.

25. Part of a large mural made from jute, unspun fiber, and yarn of various weights. These materials were adhered to soft board and were then sprayed with Hyplar (PVA) to achieve a stiff sculptural finish. Figure 74 shows the total mural.

26. Photographs of beached tree trunks whose bark has been removed by the action of waves. Note the color and texture where the trunks have been bleached by the sun and in some cases burned.

26

26

27

Forests, Groves and Thickets

Forests, groves, and thickets all give a sense of envelopment, of being contained in a separate and complex environment. Within these closed worlds, we observe vertical, twisting, and curved lines.

27. Tree branches creating curved linear forms.

28. Trees in a rain forest, when hung with moss, take on a unique aspect — an interplay of curved and vertical lines.

29
30

29. Strong vertical lines and a broken effect of light and shade upon trunks and stems often characterize forests and groves. The textile designs shown here incorporate some of these elements.

30. The vertical quality of this work has been influenced by the linear quality of trees. Black sewing cotton and other materials have been trapped between two layers of Plexiglas (perspex) so the thread will retain its basic linear quality without interlacement of any sort.

31. A three-piece textile work (20' x 12') which hangs at an office window. The technique is macrame knotting with ¾" diameter white polypropylene rope.

32. **Triple Banner,** soft cotton rope, uses only the overhand and larkshead knots.

33D. Detail of **Triple Banner.**

31

32

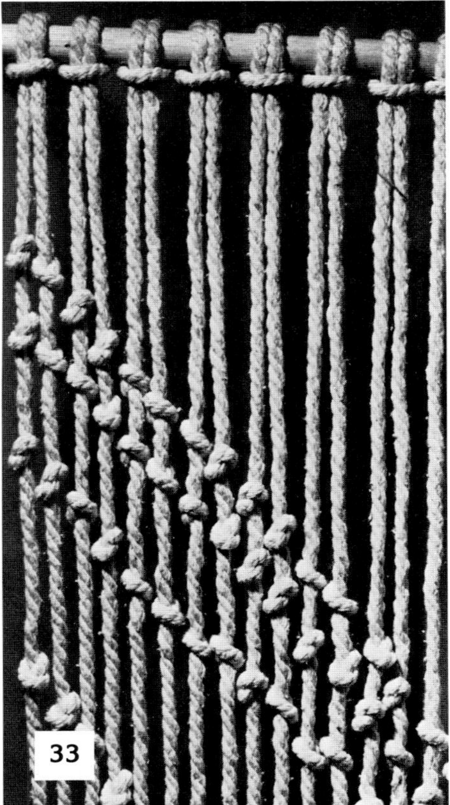

33

Reeds and Grasses

Reeds and grasses have several different decorative elements within them. One characteristic is verticality, a thrusting upwards, and a sense of growth. Another is their strong yet delicate, linear qualities which become most apparent when they are silhouetted or struck with a strong light. Still another is the infinite variety and characteristics of the seed heads. (Figures 34).

35. This handwoven and embroidered altar frontal contains grasses in order to achieve a sense of growth and verticality. Grasses and verticality were necessary for two reasons: 1) the viewer's eye to rise naturally to a large embroidery on the sanctuary wall and 2) the sanctuary is in a temporary chapel installed yearly in an agricultural show. The grasses were woven in as weft with the seed heads left free (in the photograph, weft is vertical to us). The altar cloth is of acrylic fabric which launders well and is excellent for "pulled work" embroidery because of its firm, open quality.

36D. Detail of woven altar frontal.

37D. Detail of embroidered altar cloth.

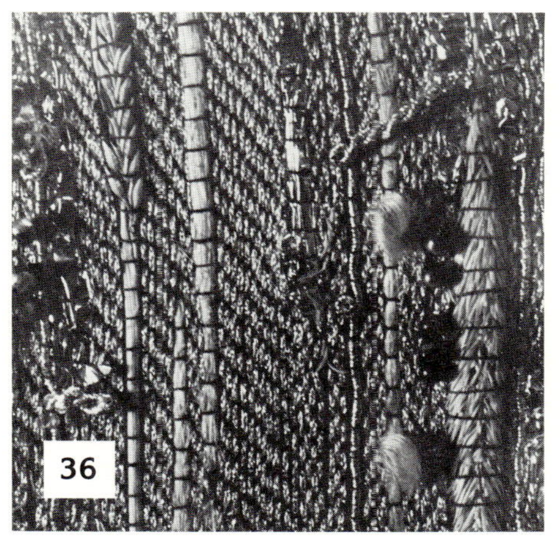

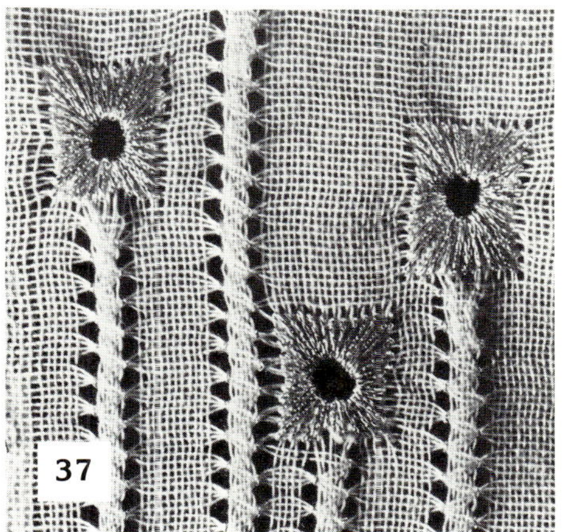

38. Threads and other elements are held between layers of Plexiglas (perspex) in this close-up of a three-dimensional textile piece. A different section of this wall hanging appears in Figure 30.

39. Machine embroidery on printed terylene net stretched over Plexiglas and framed.

Mountains and Sky

When experiencing the unfamiliar, we tend to see things as they are and not how we assume them to be. Flying, in particular, brings one into an awareness of shapes, colors, and patterns not seen everyday.

40–41. In these photographs of mountain tops buried in deep snow, note the interplay of white on white, the scattered nebulous shapes, the shadows, and the sense of space.

42–45. Three wall hangings were influenced by impressions of mountains, snow, and clouds. The only color used is white and the dominant materials are wool and cotton. Additional materials include strips of simulated fur, crushed silks, and velvet. It is important to light these wall hangings so that a deep shadow is created which will enhance the surface textures.

42

40

43

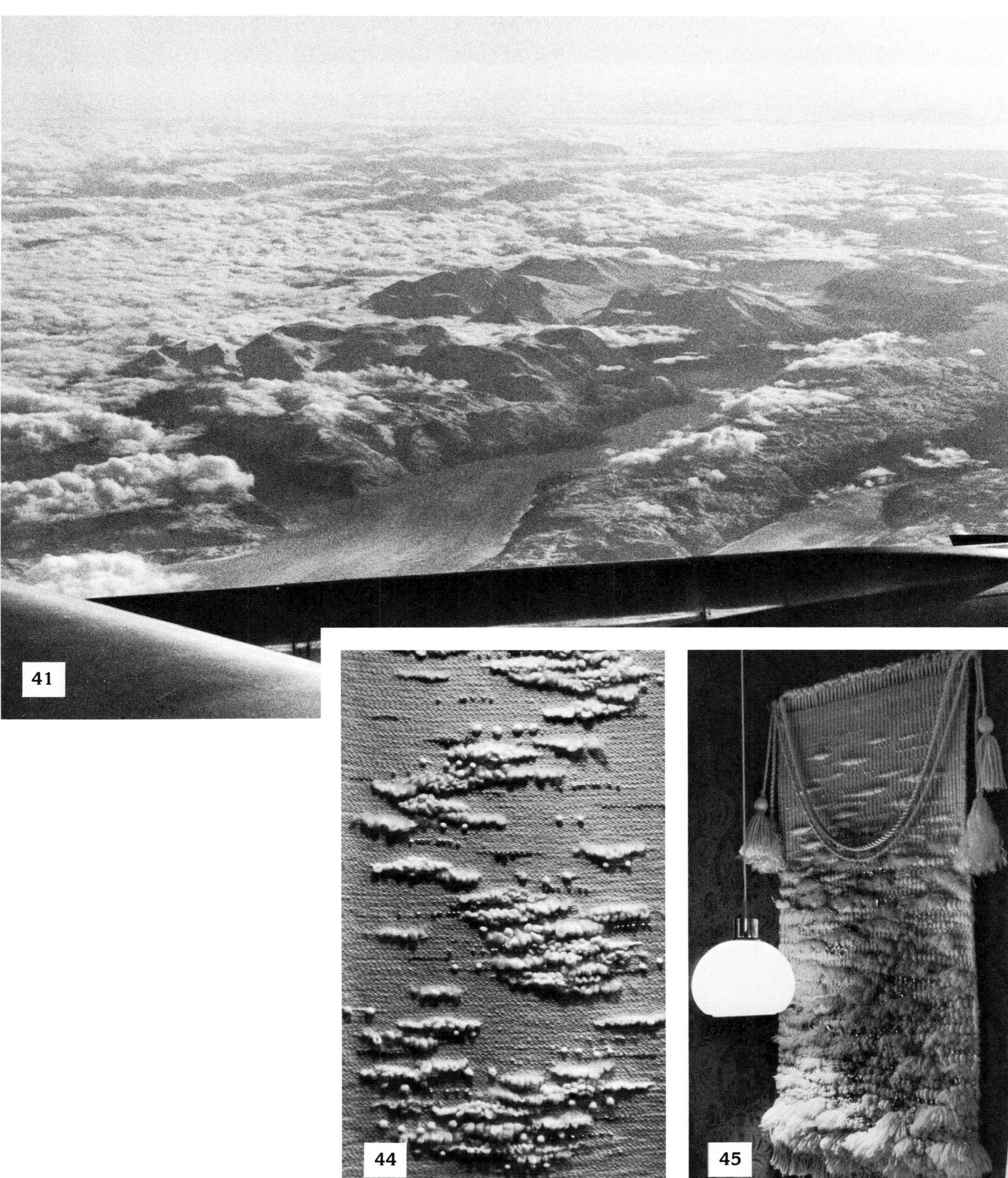
41
44
45

46

47

48

50

49

46. Three-dimensional wall hanging made for a college library. It resembles the other works influenced by mountain and snow patterns, but is more complex. In addition to the deep-texture weaving in whites, it also contains spaced-warp weaving, macrame knotting, overhand knotting, winding, braiding, and ropes — all done with whites of various shades and lusters.

47–49. In these photographs of sky and clouds, observe the nebulous, vague shapes, the merging tones and colors, and the immense subtlety of form and spatial relationships.

50–51D. This ecclesiastical stole was inspired by landscape patterns and the floating, ragged qualities of clouds. The background is a striped fabric in blues; over which area blue, gray, and silver-gray appliqué silk shapes, machine embroidered lines, large French knots and paillettes.

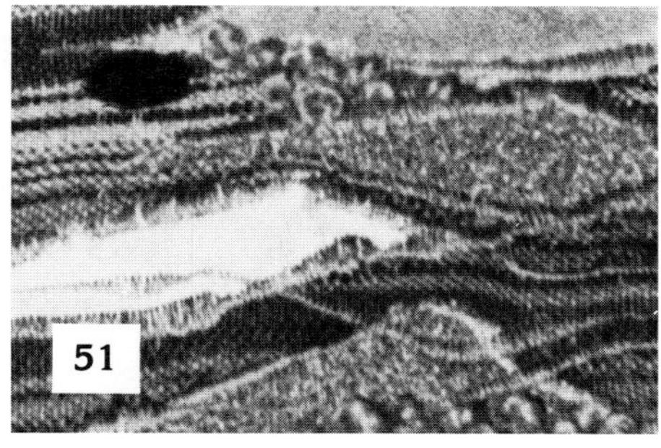

51

52

Water, Waves and Wash

Focusing our attention on the constantly changing, swirling shapes produced by water in agitation, whether from a boat or from the shore, can draw us deeper and deeper into contemplation of fluid curves. We see curves of many sizes and shapes, opening out and collapsing, composed of light froth and spume contrasted against the darker greens and blues, or, if the shore is sandy, browns.

52. The movement of the water from a boat's wash is dynamic and restless.

53–54. Waves advancing and receding on a beach create distinct arrangements of sand and stone.

53

54

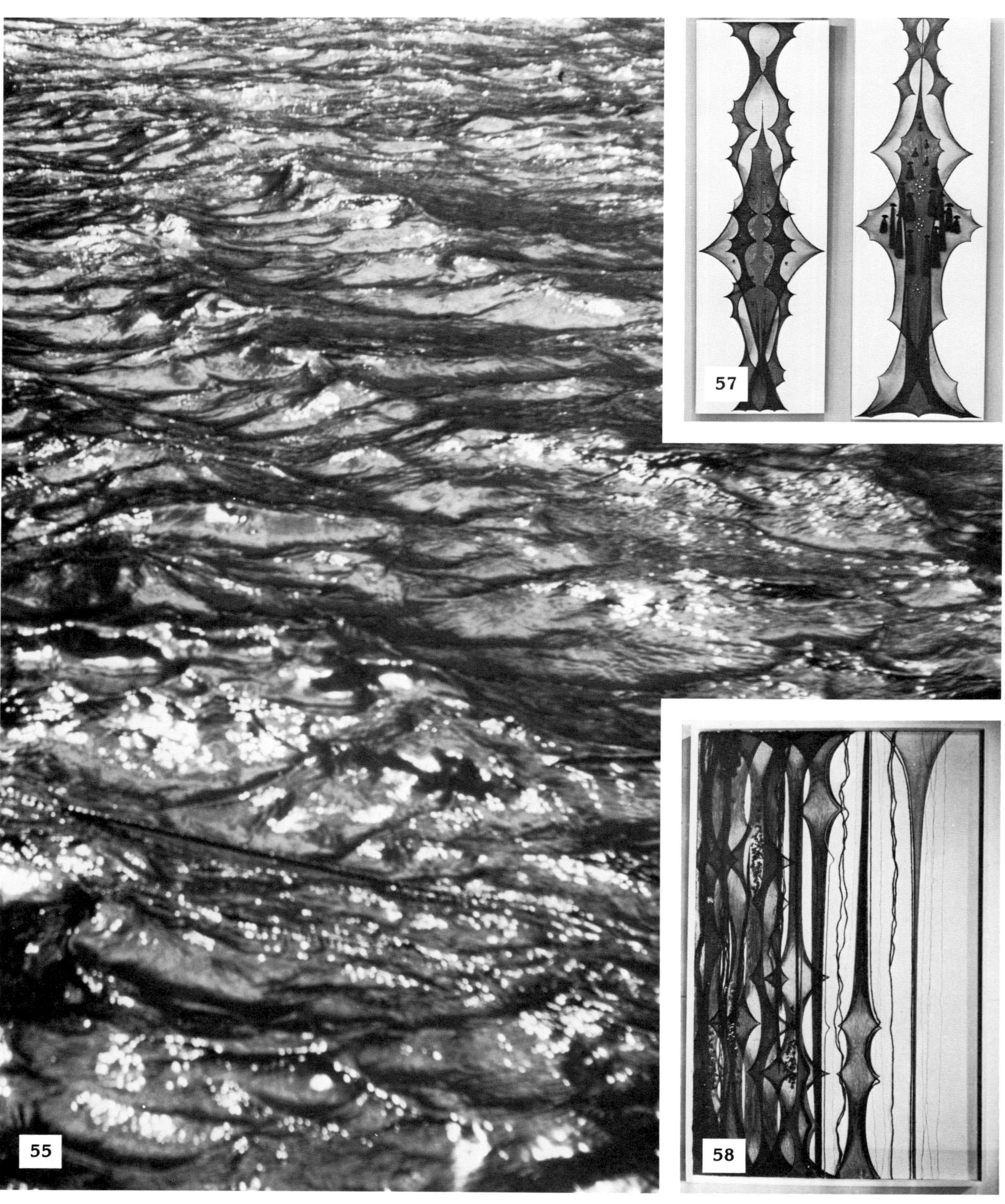
55
57
58

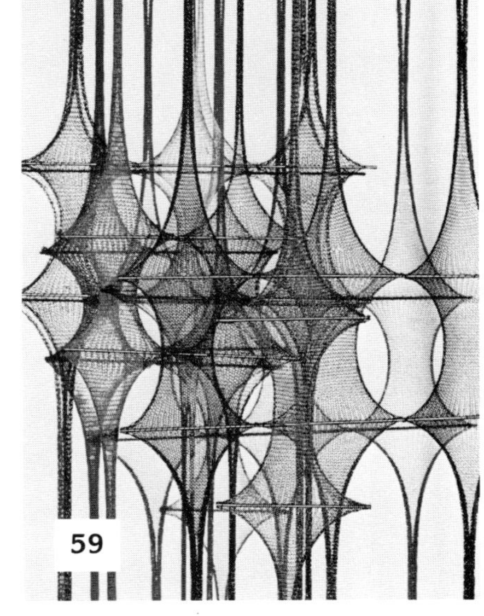

55–56. Seawater can create a variety of surface texture from intricate, broken patterns to flat airy shapes.

Textile techniques which stretch, change, and curve with fluidity are suitable for capturing the varied movement of water. Open, plain knitting produced in fine, smooth threads is one such technique. The wall hangings and panels on this page were produced in smooth, fine, nylon yarns and other fine, slippery yarns on a 7-gauge domestic knitting machine. In general, there was little shaping on the machine as the curved forms were created by stretching, holding, and fixing the fabric in various ways. Great accuracy of tension and stitch number was needed.

57–58. Two panels, each 6' x 2'. Their backgrounds are of white painted soft-board framed in wood and the fabric used is black nylon 7-gauge knitted fabric (20" wide x 8'6" long of straight knitting, finished off with an extra 2' of decreasing to a point). The single pieces of fabric were folded, stretched, folded back on themselves, and twisted. Points are secured with fine, short pins. This is a very flexible method of working as shapes can be changed at will. When the shapes are satisfactory, a small dab of transparent adhesive (Hyplar) secures each pinhead. The same technique and fabric has been used in the landscape panel (4' x 2'6"), but the black is softened by ochres and browns. The knitted strips vary in width and some decrease to a point. Threads of various thickness are added and minute texture is achieved by means of black hooks and eyes.

59. Three-dimensional space-hanging, composed of several layers of stretched, knitted strips with no decreasing whatsoever. The strips are stretched on stainless steel rods, stitched together, and secured to the ends of the rods with adhesive.

60. Stairhanging, composed of two different sized panels which hang 2" from the wall. Each panel contains 5 strips of straight knitting. Colors are ochre, greens, and khaki. This technique not only gives curved shapes but interesting tonal density, depending upon how much the fabric is stretched.

61

62

Seaweeds

Seaweeds static on rocks and beaches and seaweeds moving in their natural element, water, have very different characteristics. Seaweed, lying heaped or scattered without movement, has a three-dimensional globular, broken quality. Weed agitated by water often has a more sinuous linear quality.

63

64
66

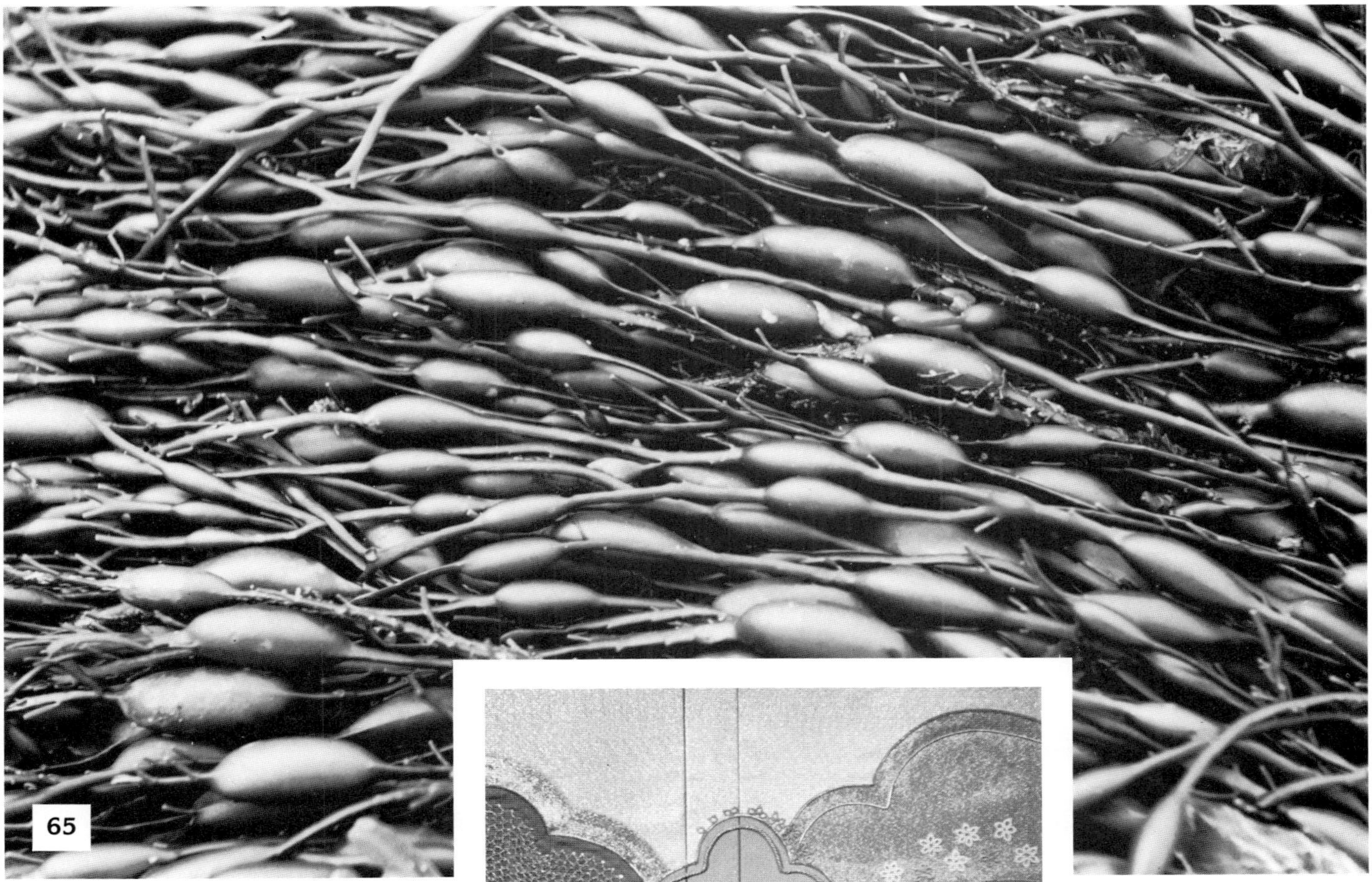

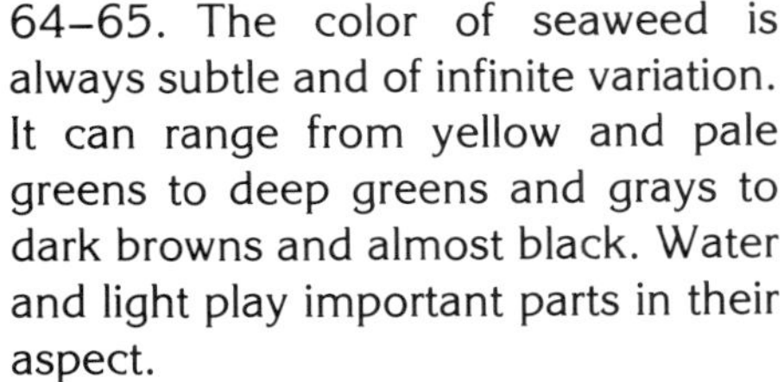

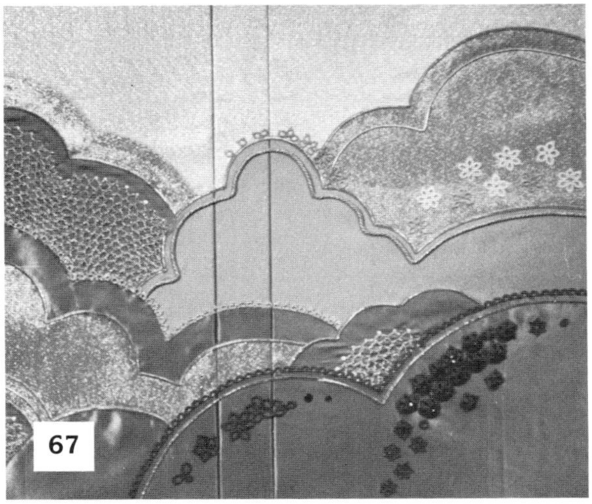

64–65. The color of seaweed is always subtle and of infinite variation. It can range from yellow and pale greens to deep greens and grays to dark browns and almost black. Water and light play important parts in their aspect.

66. This work was derived from the encrusted quality of seaweed and limpets on rocks and was made by tatting — a specialized form of knotting — in a rough, gold thread. The tatted rondels were deliberately formed with fewer rings than usual in order to make three-dimensional, rather than flat, shapes.

67. In this segmented mural, the main technique is appliqué embroidery, with tatting as embellishment.

68D. Detail of segmented mural.

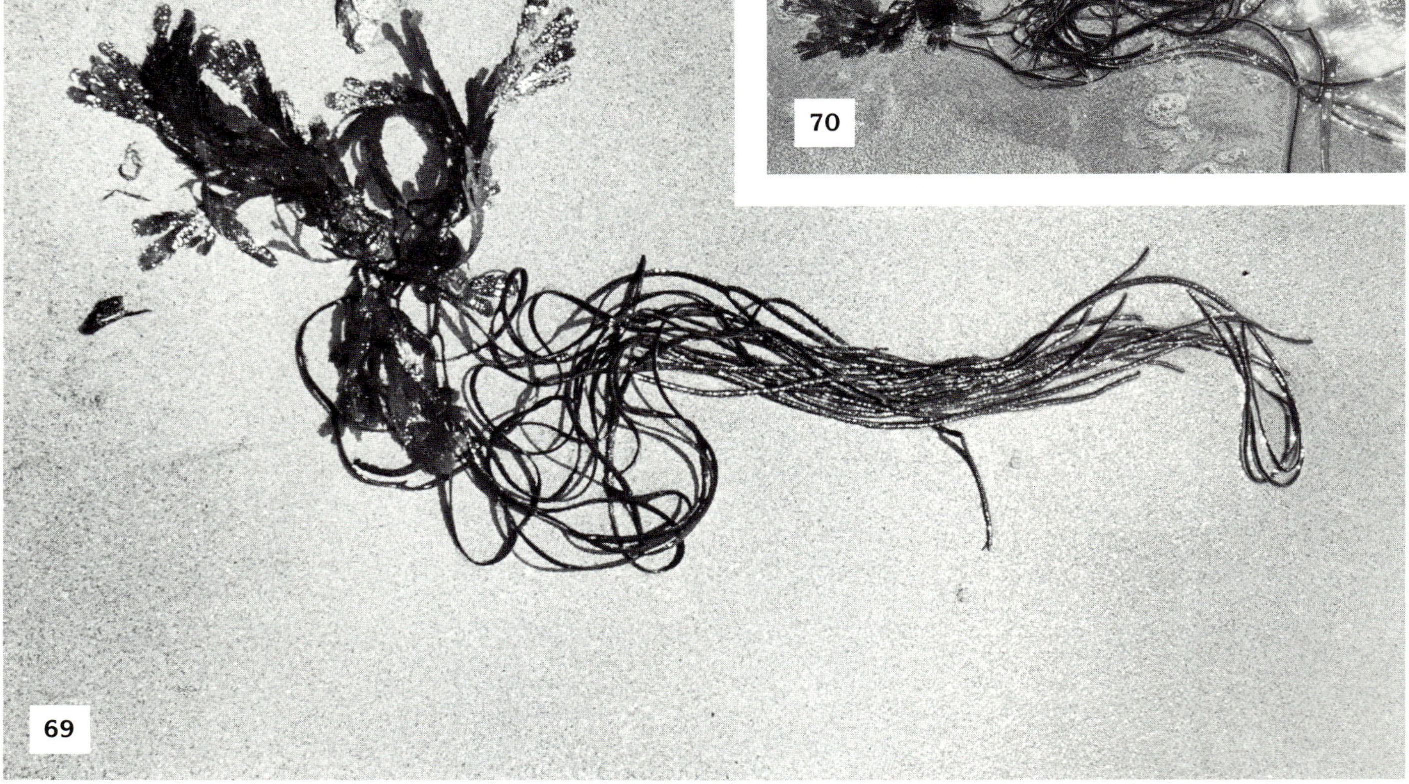

70

69

69–72. These four photographs were taken as the same piece of seaweed was washed and moved into quite different shapes by the action of successive waves. Its configurations are both sinuous and graceful.

73. In this small panel, the imagery of the curving induced by qualities of seaweed is produced in tatted shapes with a fairly thick silk thread on burlap (Hessian) ground.

74. This large mural (4' x 12') was created for a realtor's office. Worked on soft-board with jute yarn and fiber, it flows across the wall to create a sense of ease and space.

73

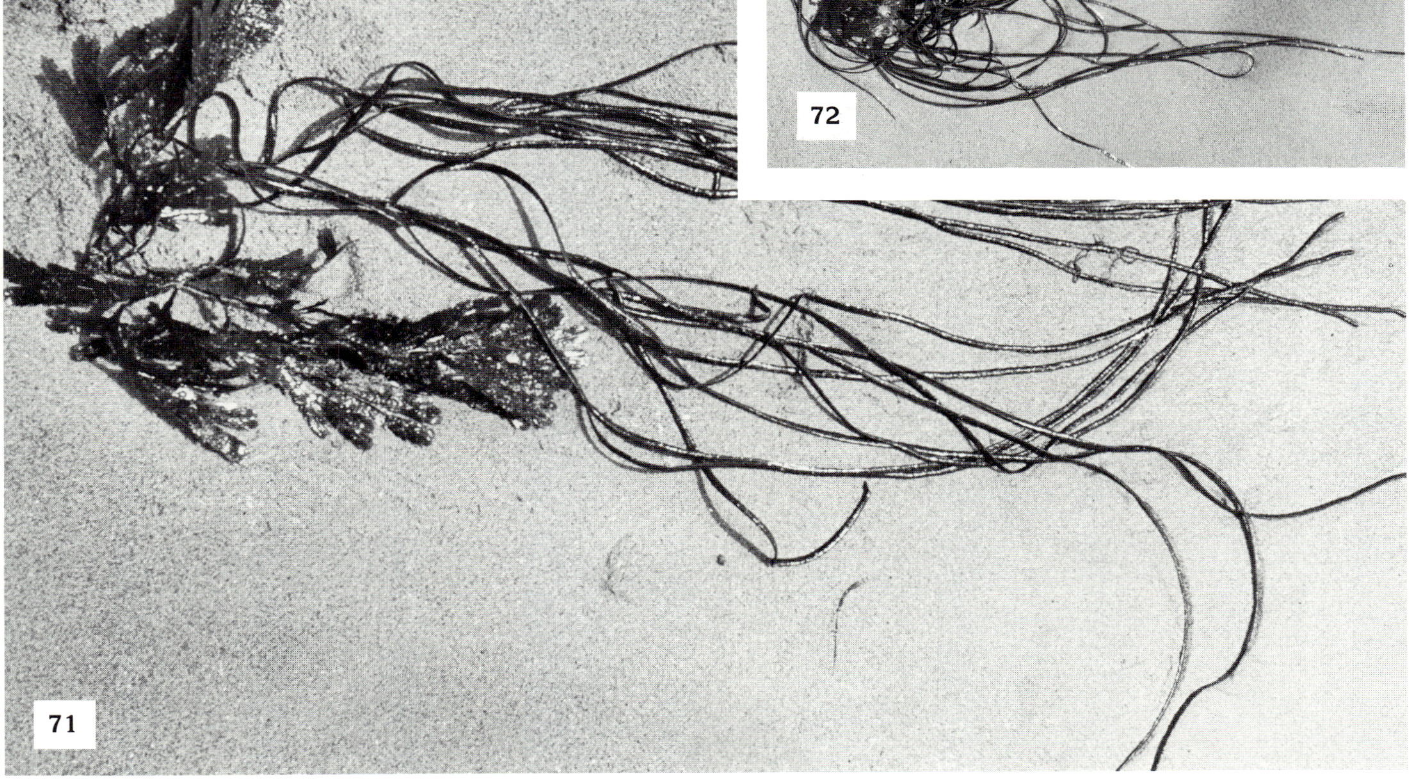

72

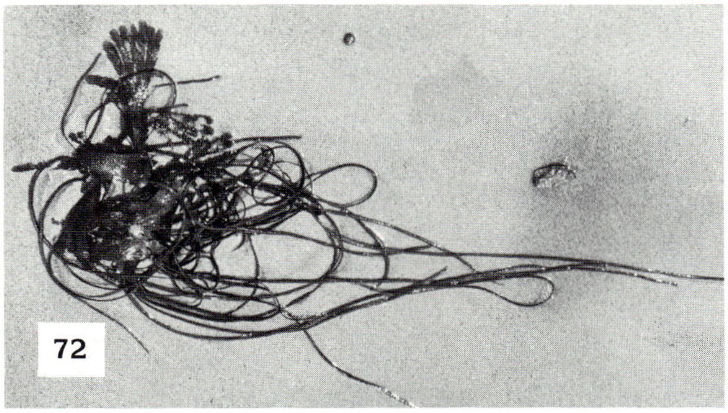

71

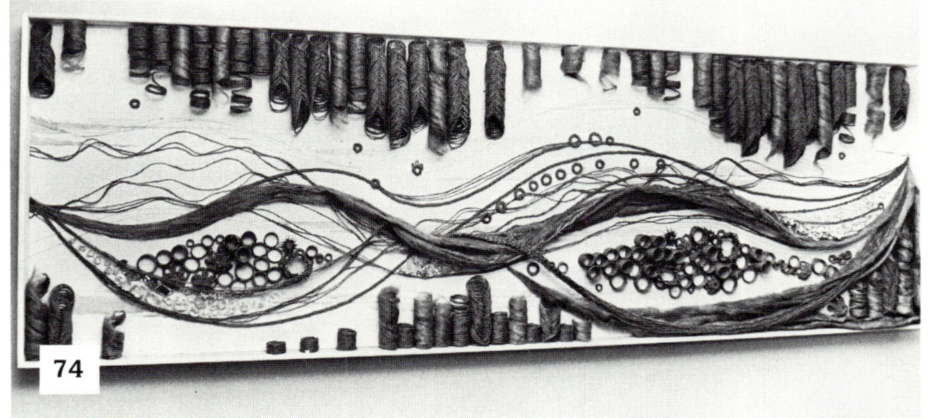

74

75

75. Seaweed lying on the shore often becomes entangled with debris, which can yield unexpected beauty. The textures and lines of artificial objects against natural elements can create unusual patterns. The flat, dark, straight, and angular lines of this abandoned fire-guard contrasts strikingly with the light, textural curves of the seaweed.

76–77. Two altar frontals, both somewhat influenced by debris on the shore contrasted with natural forms.

78D. In this frontal, small clusters of richness contrast with areas of lesser texture which have been broken up with lines. In addition to presenting textured against smooth surfaces, this frontal was designed to incorporate some of the vertical feeling in the carving behind the altar.

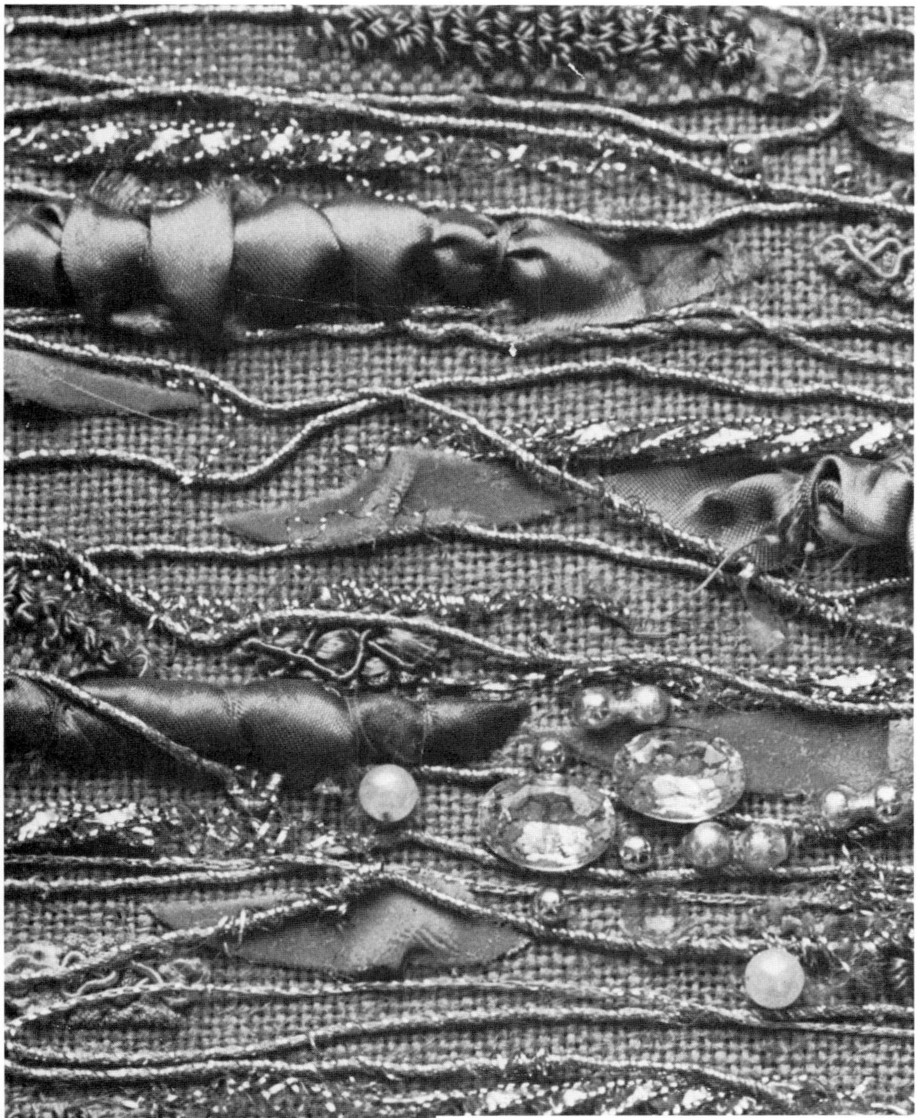

76

77

78

Nets and Ropes

Nets and ropes are both of tremendous visual interest for their pattern, texture, and sinuosity. Nets fall into flowing, curving shapes because the technique by which they are made has enormous capability for expanding and contracting. There is more evidence of netting around us than we sometimes realize.

79–82. Not only are there the obvious — fishing nets and the like — but hairnets, shopping bags, tennis nets, huge nets thrown over heavy goods on trailers and trucks, camouflage nets, safety nets, heavy wire nets for fences, and light wire nets for salad-shakers. Nets are both a visual stimulant and a textile technique themselves. Their very presence can lead us to use the netting technique itself as a part of our textile designs.

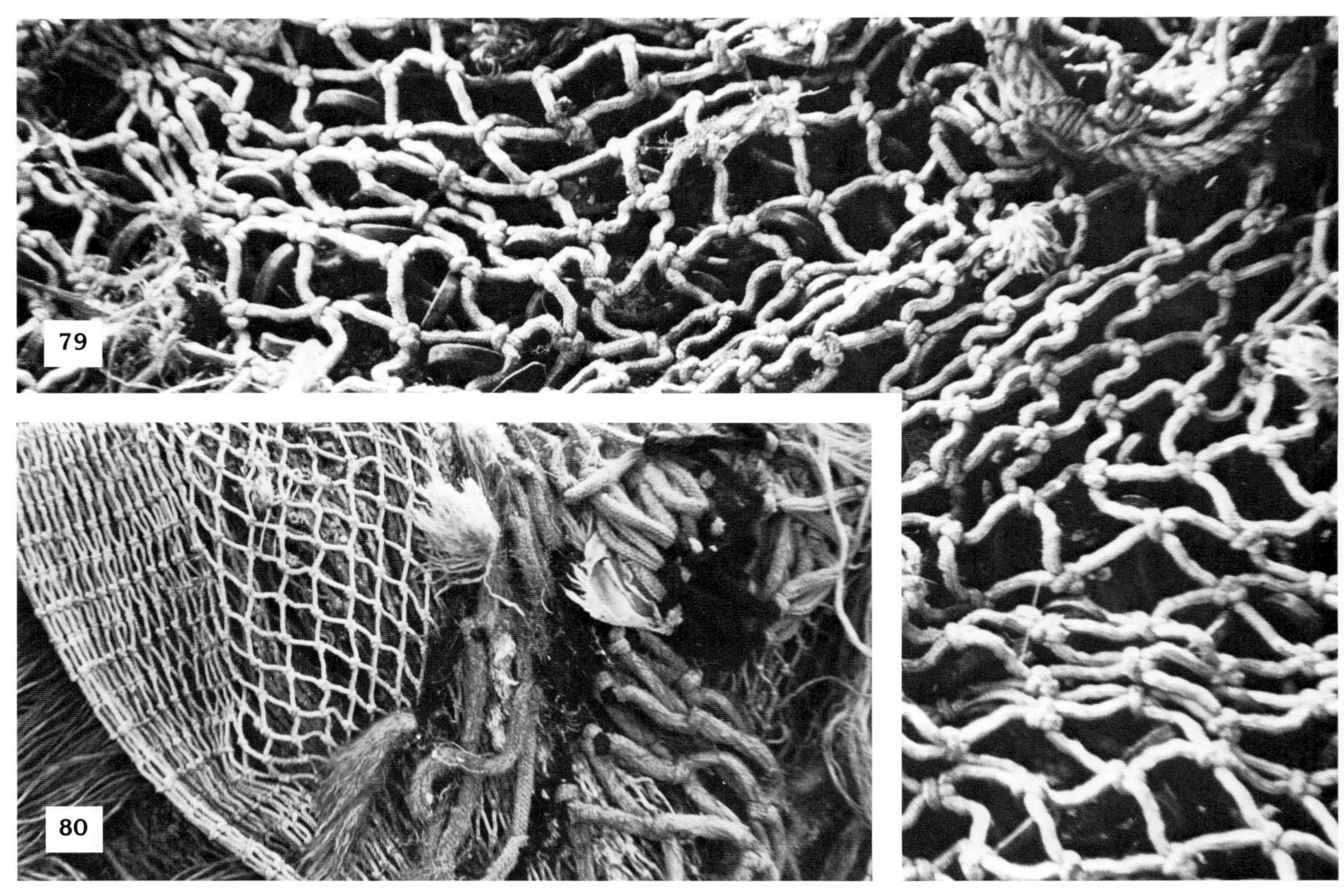

81

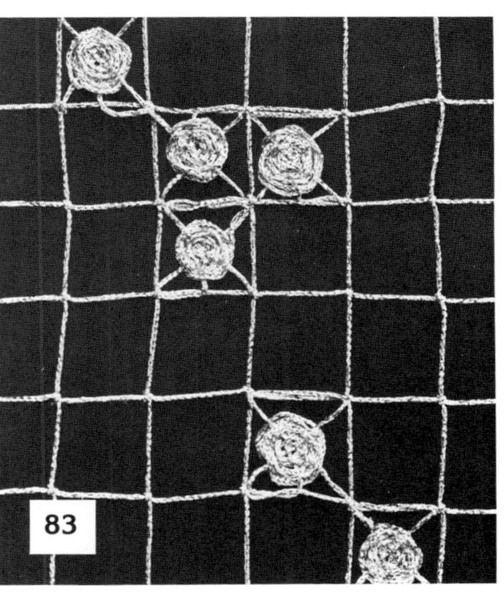

83

82

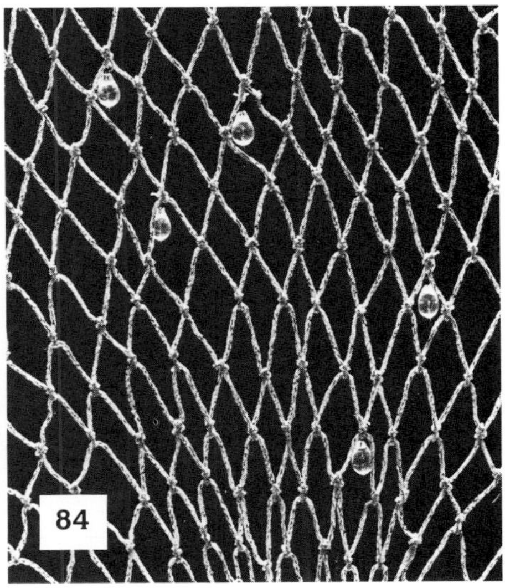

84

85–86D. The regularity of knotting inherent in net construction is exploited in this square netting made of jute. The embroidery is also jute (embroidered square netting is known as filet net).

87. Ropes, by their very nature, create thicker and heavier curves.

88. A feeling of weight and dignity is created by the wool ropes and tatted tassels on this handwoven and embroidered ecclesiastical cope.

85

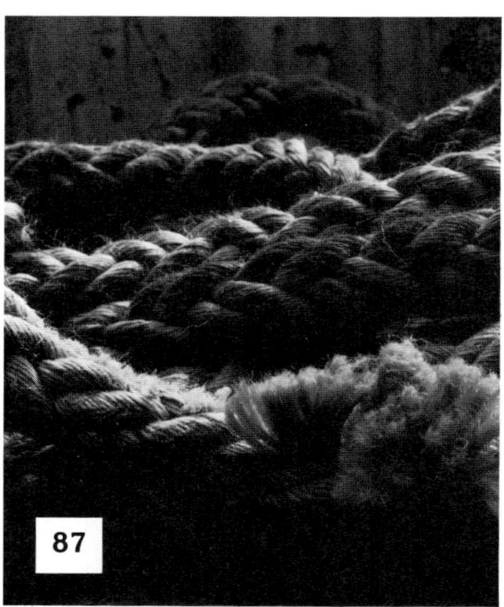
87

88

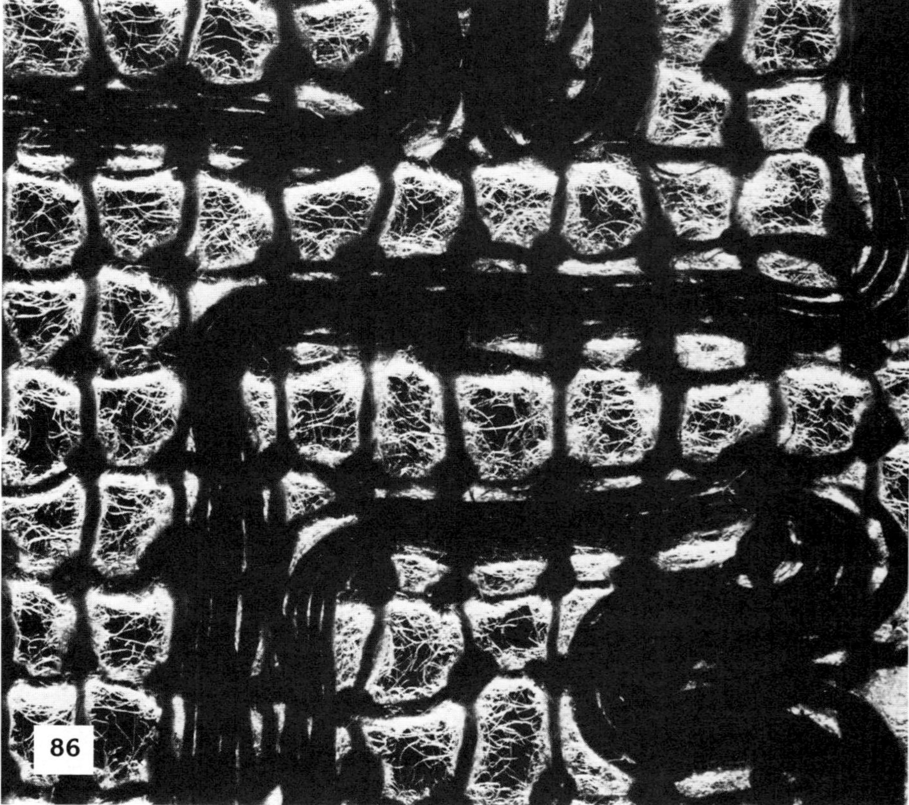
86

89

90

91

89–91D. Room divider, made entirely of woolen ropes of varying diameters in tones of brown. The problems here were two-fold: 1) to create an aesthetically satisfying and practical room divider for a show house in an exhibition, and 2) to make it in a technically simple manner so that people non-skilled in textile techniques could produce it. A national magazine featured this project for the non-specialist. Ropes were the perfect answer as the only procedure is to twist long bundles of threads (as in this case wool) in the same direction as they are already twisted and to double them. The result is a tight twist which stays in place. The room divider was given weight and finish with tassels.

92
93
94
95
96

Architecture

Modern architecture is full of vast pattern — both linear and mass. Its exteriors and interiors can provoke a variety of textile ideas.

92–94. Roofs, for example, have regular or irregular repeating patterns. Overlapping is often crucial to their construction. At times, their patterns are softened and broken up by growths that form on their surfaces.

95. This miniature, made of long pile embroidery in fine threads, features an element of broken overlapping.

96D. Detail

While we readily discern repeating patterns in roofs, we rarely do in damp and decaying surfaces.

97. Each inch of this decaying wall is unique, yet, the whole is composed of cohesive elements.

98–99. The broken plaster on these walls creates contrasting areas of flatness and high texture.

100–101. Undulating tones and textures can be seen in decaying pillars.

97

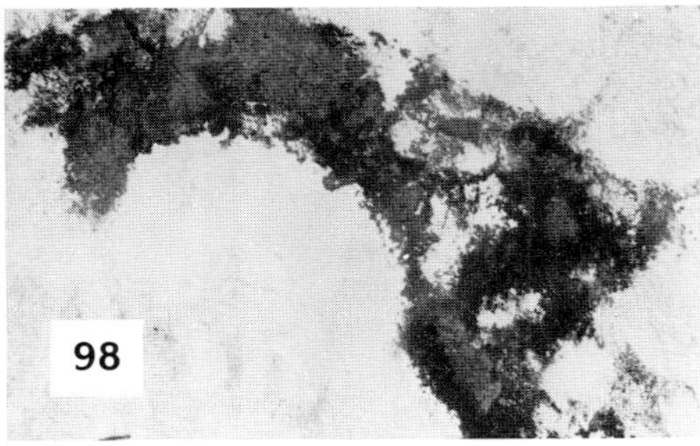

98

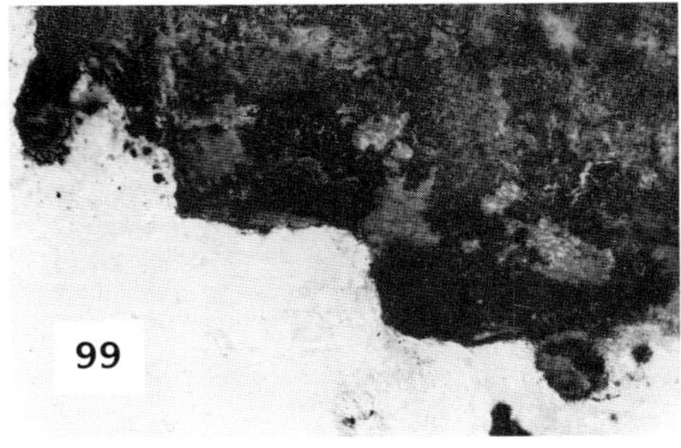

99

100

101

102

102–103. Modern buildings impress us with their massiveness and strong, linear qualities. The visual opportunities they offer for pattern-making are endless.

104. An obvious pattern is striping seen in this wound-thread maquette for a wall hanging.

105. Seen en masse, modern buildings become pattern against pattern — a visual concept worth developing in our designs.

106. This old railway station, in contrast to modern architecture, is full of decorative pattern in its wood and iron finishings.

107

Standing Objects

Standing objects — from those we make to those we find in our natural environment — provide intriguing shapes and surface patterns.

107–109. Tombs and gravestones are interesting not only for their own shapes and decorative surfaces but also for their relationship to the setting in which they appear.

110–112. Pillars and columns often resemble the tree trunks from which they were originally fashioned. They are vertical, soar or twist upwards, and have massive strength and bulk.

108

109

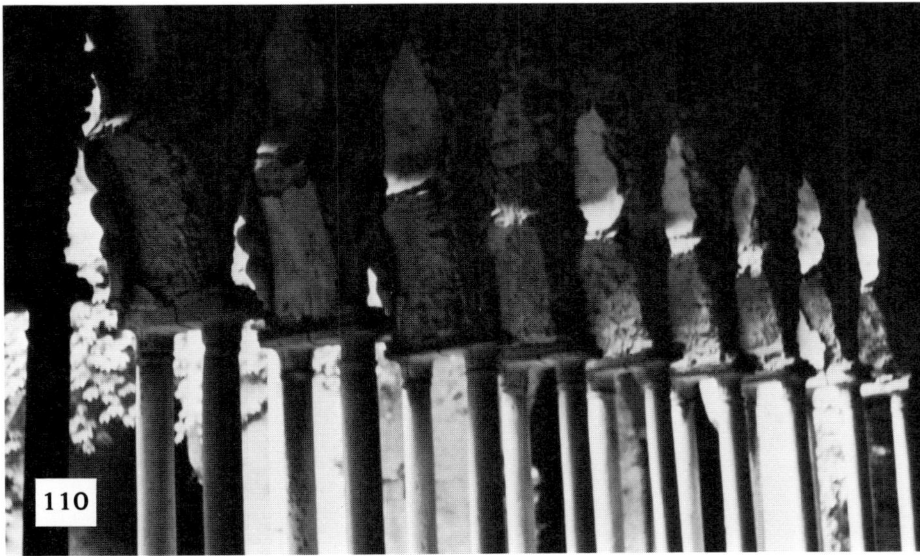
110

111

113–114. Pillars inspired this woven tapestry, stiff because of the tapestry woven wefts of thick wools, sturdy cords, braids, and clear acetate strip. Because of this stiffness, the weave forms firm, convex shapes easily. The "pillars" are also visually anchored to the ground on which they stand by the breaking up and thickening of the surface toward the bases with ropes and pile.

115–117D. This work, entitled **Group of Five,** was partially inspired by images of columns. Its massive quality, verticality, and repetitiveness suggest a colonnade. Yet its weave — of which the five elements are made — results from the sculptured behavior of loosely spun, thick jute yarn when woven on a widely spaced warp.

112

113

114

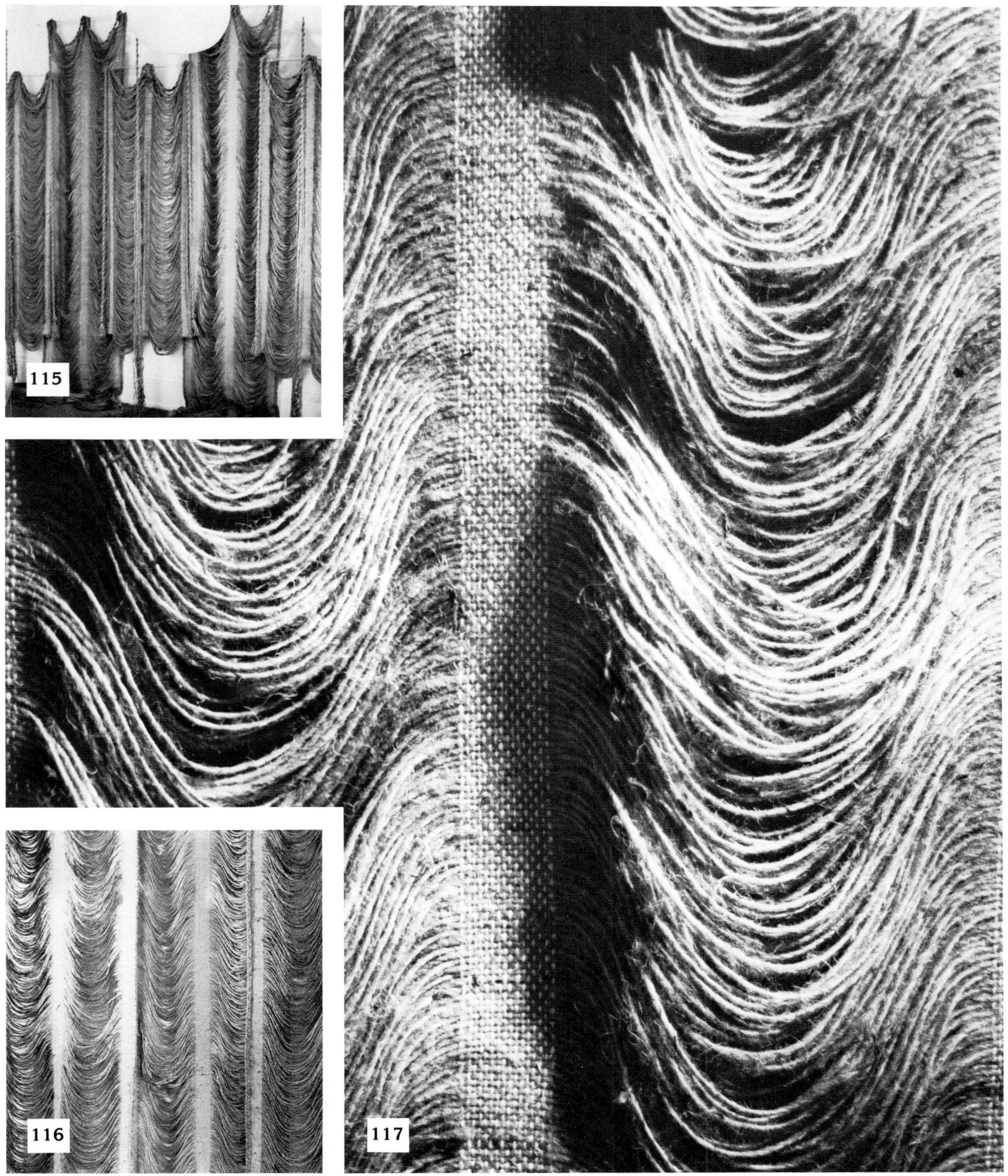
115
116
117

120

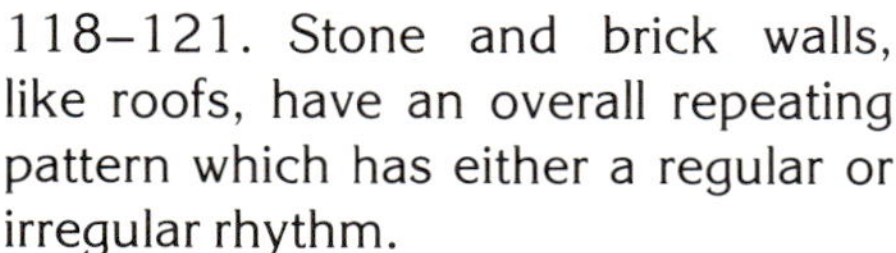

118–121. Stone and brick walls, like roofs, have an overall repeating pattern which has either a regular or irregular rhythm.

122–123. This design was influenced by patterns perceived in walls and masonry. It is a heavy, hand-knitted work which was built up in a bricklike sequence and has the hexagonal, three-dimensional appearance of dressed stone.

123

122

124

127

125

124–126. Fences and fortifications are dominated by the same strong verticals as groves and forests. Their more detailed features depend upon the material of which they are made and the purpose for which they were built.

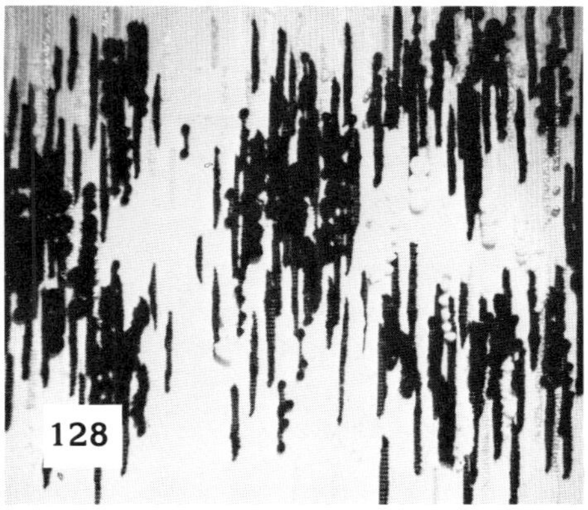

127. Design for a rug, in mock-up form, based on broken fences seen in snow.

128. This mural (3' x 6') is hand-woven and employs the same techniques described on page 27.

129. Stones are hard, three-dimensional objects which have been rounded by the action of weather and abrasion for millions of years. This work was inspired by the stones and worn stone crosses that litter the north-west European landscape. It is "soft sculpture" made of burlap and embellished with jute cords, threads, and gold textures.

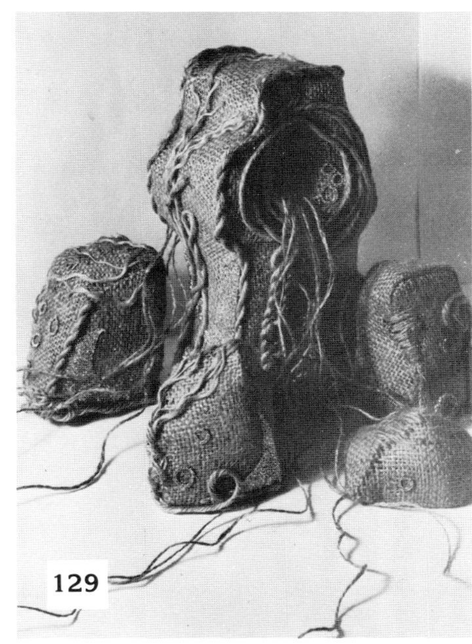

Small Textures

From the immensity of modern architecture to the intricacy of plants and pebbles, all have texture in common. Tiny, varied textures abound in our environment. Lichens, for example, are on almost every rock and stone surface whether the rock is still in its natural form or has been fashioned into something else.

130–132. These small, encrusted growths are generally rounded and full of color.

133–135. Their colors range from black to green, yellow, orange, and white.

136. Rock plants, with circular fleshy leaves, catch light and create provocative circular rhythms.

137–142. Other sources of varied, intricate texture are leaves, a stone-faced house facade, old scaling stone blocks and broken Roman brickwork, flint and stone set in cement, and limpet encrusted stones.

143–144. Two portions of pieces of work, both tatting, deliberately irregular in formation and constructed of lustrous and rich threads. They represent a world of small textures.

131

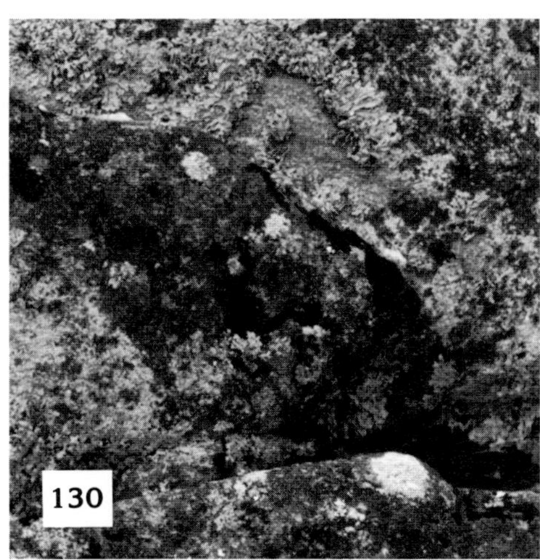

130

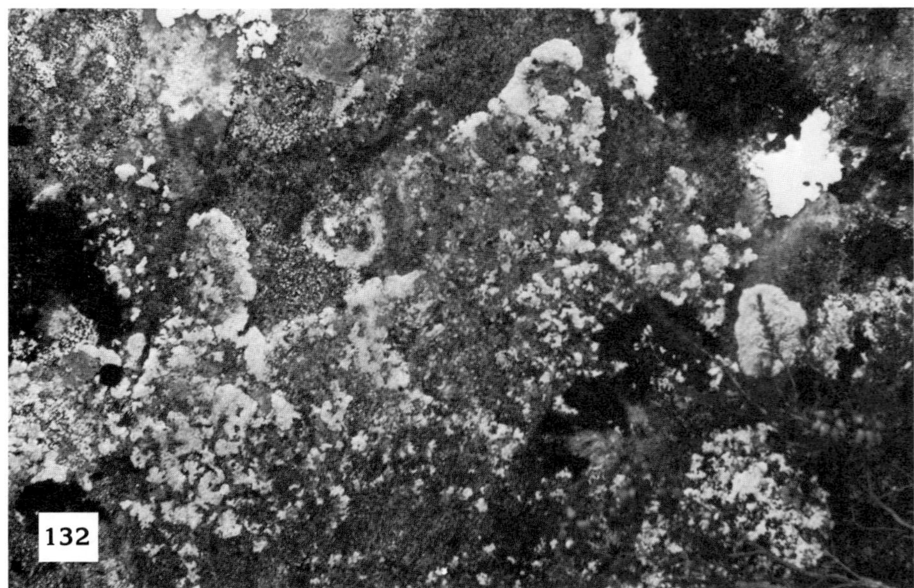

132

133
143
134

135
144
136

137
138
139
140
141
142

145

Radiating Forms

Many things radiate from a central point — the sun's rays seen through breaks in clouds and the lines of crystals seen under a microscope.

145. In this close-up of a center of a yucca plant, its radiating lines are delineated by the pinpoints of light at the serrated edges of the leaves.

146. A radiating image is created in this collage with chunks of various metals, fabrics, threads, and beads on open burlap (Hessian) ground. Silver foil lies under the burlap. Colors are black, gray, and silver.

147. In this collage, threads radiate from a central ring and on a stretched fabric ground. The threads — a rayon and metal twist — have a very special and lively characteristic; requiring no other ornamentation than themselves.

148–149D. This panel is produced in wools, jute fiber, and fiberglass. Its pile is stapled to a wooden board backing and its colors are natural, silver, and white.

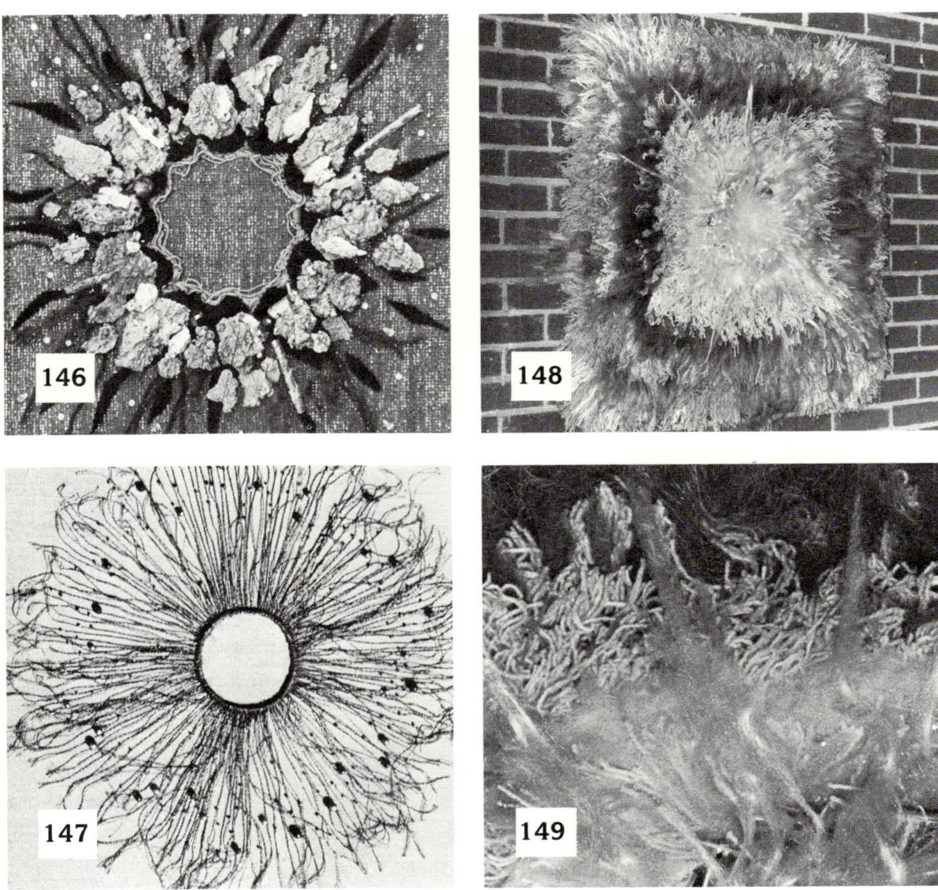

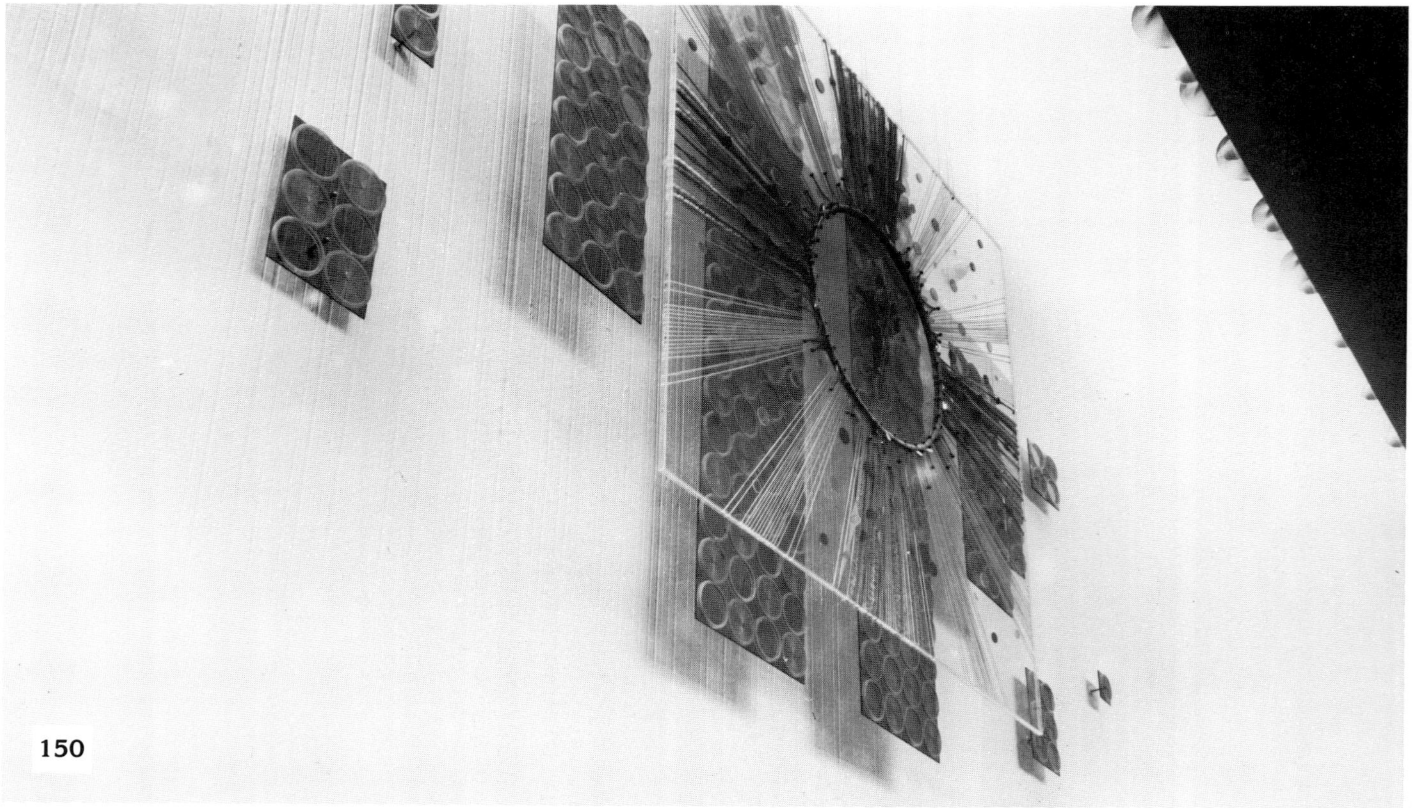

150

151

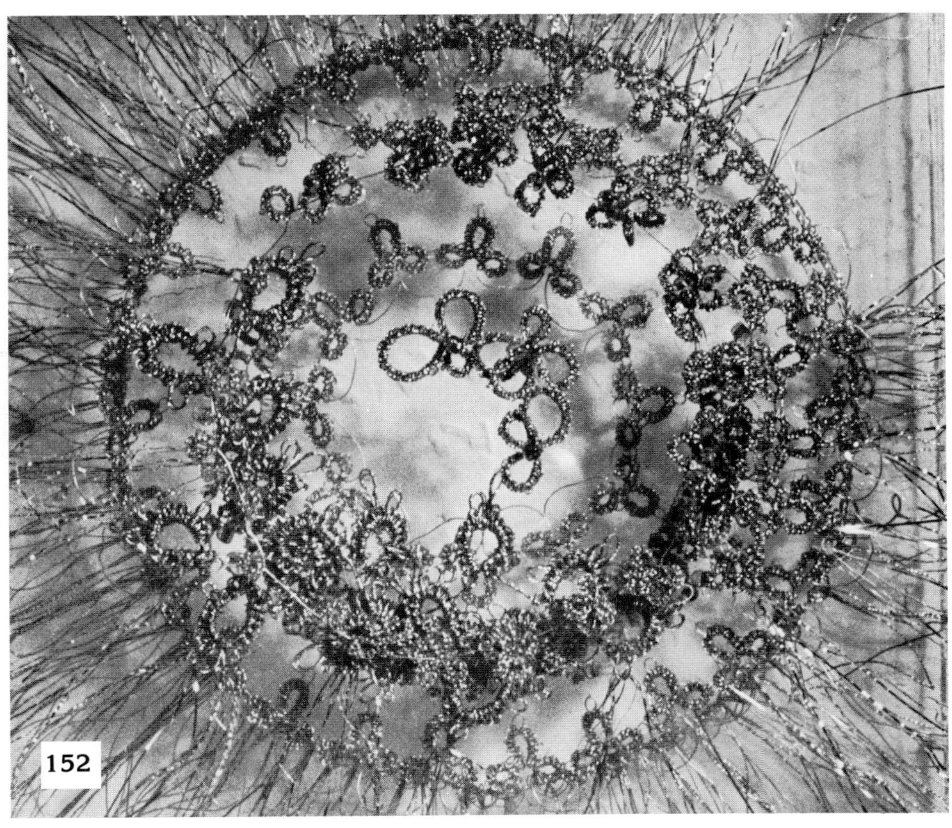

150–151D. This mural for a sanctuary wall is made of thread on Plexiglas. Linear radiation is used to a considerable extent both in the center panel and in the treatment of the ground circles.

152. Miniature of tatted gold thread, set in layers of Plexiglas.

153. A free hanging thread-and-Plexiglas cross incorporates the principle of radiating form.

Pattern and Light

Striking patterns are commonly detected in ordinary objects, particularly when seen out of context.

154. Stacked flat cardboard boxes create a provocative image of order.

155. Paper sacks create interesting pattern. Observed pattern is suggested by the physical material which forms an object. We also see pattern because of the different kinds of light which play on an object's surface.

154

155

156

157

158

156. River logs and grasses sharply delineated by bright sunlight, strong shadows, and contrasts of light and dark.

157. Rows of canisters show the effect of the interplay of light and dark. Certain shapes, such as the circular lids and the rectangular tops, receive emphasis because they are highlighted against a dark mass.

158–159. Sharp contrasts of strong shadows alone create exciting patterns. A study of intricate shadow patterns. Tonal contrasts of light and dark combine with decorative exchange of solid, geometric shapes and their fluid echoes.

159

160

160. Reflections can also create pattern as seen in this image of a hydroelectric plant reflected in water on the highway.

161–164. Subtle gradations of color and tone can add depth and richness to simple contrasts of light and dark. Compare how the tonal contrasts in these pictures affect our responses.

161

162

163

164

Design Sources

References to the geographical location of design sources was deliberately omitted. It is really not relevant where the sources are located; it is more important to note how they have been used. It may, however, be interesting to note some of the locations: Hidecote Manor Gardens, Gloucestershire; Trescoe Abbey Gardens, Scilly Islands; Devon, Scotland, and St. Fagans, South Wales - all in the United Kingdom; Paestum, Capri, Ravello, Pompeii in Italy; Vancouver, Edmonton and Ontario, Canada; and the states of Washington, Michigan and New Jersey in the United States.

Textile Works

Pg. 24. Silver altar frontal, embroidered. 6'x 3'. (Figure 13.)

Pg. 24 Gold altar frontal, embroidered. Cradley Heath Parish Church, West Midlands, England. (Figure 14-15).

Pg. 26. Gold altar frontal, woven and embroidered. St. Peters Church, Kinver, Staffordshire, England. (Figure 18-19).

Pg. 27. Mural, woven and embroidered. Birmingham Post & Mail Building. (Figure 20-21).

Pg. 28. **Looking Glass Tree,** embroidered panel. Collection of Dr. & Mrs. Chris Heyward, Warwickshire, England. (Figure 23-24).

Pg. 28. Detail of mural for Evans, Jennings & Talbot, Droitwich Spa, Worcestershire, England. (Figure 25, also 74).

Pg. 33. Interior of macrame window hanging for B.H.P. Machine Tools Ltd., Aldridge, Staffordshire, England. (Figure 31).

Pg. 33. **Triple Knotted Banner.** Collection of Mrs. Marriott, Aldridge Staffordshire, England. (Figure 32-33).

Pg. 35. Close-up of Plexiglas (perspex) and thread panels, 5' x 4' x 1'6".

Pg. 34-35. Woven and embroidered altar frontal and pulled-work altar cloth for the Church of England Chapel at the Royal Agricultural Show, Stoneleigh, Kenilworth, Warwickshire, England. (Figure 35-37).

Pg. 35. Embroidered panel on Plexiglas (perspex), 4' x 1'10". Collection Mr. & Mrs. L. Griffin, Kidderminster, England. (Figure 39).

Pg. 36. **Day,** woven wallhanging, 4'6" x 2'. Collection of Bob Neil. (Figure 42-43).

Pg. 37. Woven wallhanging photographed in an interior scheme at the Ideal Home Exhibition, London. Collection of Dr. Bertha Kemp, Somerset, England. (Figure 44).

Pg. 37. **Canadian Landscape,** woven wallhanging, 4'6" x 3'. Collection of Mrs. Anoder, Cardiff, Wales. (Figure 45).

Pg. 38. Three-dimensional multi-technique wallhanging for the Library of Dudley College of Education, West Midlands, England. (Figure 46).

Pg. 39. Stole, machine-embroidered. Property of Reverend Norman Fox, Huddersfield, England. (Figure 50-51).

Pg. 42. **King**, 6' x 2' panel, knitted fabric on painted soft-board. Collection of Dr. & Mrs. Salmon, Toronto, Canada. (Figure 57). **Queen**, same technique.

Pg. 42. **Landscape,** 4'6" x 2'6", knitted fabrics and threads on softboard. Collection of Mr. & Mrs. Tom Lisher, Cambridge, England. (Figure 58).

Pg. 43. Knitted space-hanging. (Figure 59).

Pg. 43. Stairhangings. Collection of Mr. & Mrs. Fletcher, Trimpley, Worcestershire, England. (Figure 60).

Pg. 46. Tatting, close-up of sample piece. (Figure 66).

Pg. 47. Total and detail of mural in applique and tatting for the rear of an antique shop window. Collection Mrs. Bamber, Kidderminster, England. (Figure 67-68).

Pg. 48. Tatted panel. Property of Mr. & Mrs. Payne, Berryham, England. (Figure 73).

Pg. 56. Miniature wallhanging, 10" x 5". Collection of Dorothea Krak, USA. (Figure 95-96).

Pg. 51. One of two gold altar frontals, woven and embroidered. Aberdare Crematorium, S. Wales. (Figure 76).

Pg. 51. Total and detail of gold altar frontal, woven and embroidered. Church of St. John the Evangelist, Hamilton, Ontario, Canada. (Figure 77-78).

Pg. 53. Filet net (sample piece). (Figure 83).

Pg. 53. Beaded netting. (Figure 84).

Pg. 54. Jute filet net. (Figure 85-86).

Pg. 54. Handwoven and embroidered cope (details). Property of Reverend Donald Watson, St. Peters Church, Kinver, Staffordshire. (Figure 88).

Pg. 55. Woolen rope room divider for **Living Magazine's** show-house in the **Ideal Home** Exhibition, London 1977. Also featured in the magazine as a project for readers to make for themselves. (Figure 89-91).

Pg. 59. Maquette for woven striping. (Figure 104).

Pg. 64. Total and detail of **Twin Pillars,** woven, three-dimensional wall-piece, 6'6" x 4'6". (Figure 113-114).

Pg. 65. Total and detail of **Group of Five,** three-dimensional woven hanging in jute, 13' x 6'6" x 1'. (Figure 115-117).

Pg. 67. Total and detail of **Grey Lozenge.** Hanging, knitted in sections with 4 or 6 thicknesses of carpet yarn. (Figure 122-123).

Pg. 68. Maquette for a pile rug. (Figure 127).

Pg. 69. **Black Ice,** woven panel, 6' x 3', executed in the USA and in the collection of Maria Mancuso, Rochester, New York. (Figure 128).

Pg. 69. **Stones,** soft-sculpture in jute. Collection of Mr. & Mrs. Farebrother, Burntwood, Staffordshire, England. (Figure 129).

Pg. 71-72. Tatting (sample pieces). (Figure 143-144).

Pg. 75. Collage panel, 2' x 2'. Owned by Mr. & Mrs. Michael Pearks, Walsall England. (Figure 146).

Pg. 75. Embroidered panel, 1'6" x 1'6". (Figure 147).

Pg. 75. Fiber panel, 3' x 3'. Owned by Mr. & Mrs. S. Harris, Kinver, Staffordshire, England. (Figure 148-149).

Pg. 76. Total and detail of Plexiglas (perspex) and thread mural for Weoley Castle Community Church, Birmingham, England, (Figure 150-151).

Pg. 77. Miniature, 10" square, gold thread, tatting and Plexiglas. Collection of Dr. Bertha Kemp, Somerset, England. (Figure 152).

Pg. 77. Plexiglas (perspex) and thread free-hanging cross for Harrietsham Church, Kent, England. (Figure 153).

Bibliography

Badger, Bertel. **Nature as Designer: A Botanical Art Study.** New York: Van Nostrand Reinhold Co., 1966.

Brodatz, Phil. **Textures: A Photographic Album for Artists and Designers.** New York: Dover Publishing Inc., 1966.

De Mare, Eric. **Colour Photography.** New York: Penguin Books, Inc., 1968.

______. **Photography.** New York: Penguin Books, Inc., 1957.

Feininger, Andreas. **Form in Nature and Life.** London: Thames & Hudson, 1966.

______. **The Complete Photographer.** Englewood Cliffs, New Jersey: Prentice-Hall, Inc., 1974.

______. **Total Picture Control.** Garden City, New York: American Photographic Book Publishing Co., Inc., 1970.

Fletcher, Geoffrey. **Elements of Sketching.** London: Allen and Unwin, 1967.

Friends of the Earth, Ballantine Book. **Only a Little Planet.** San Francisco.

Gerster, Georg. **Grand Design: The Earth from Above.** New York: Paddington Press Ltd., 1976.

Hedgecoe, John. **The Book of Photography.** New York: Alfred A. Knopf, Inc., 1976.

Langford, M.J. **Basic Photography.** London: Focal Press. Also, New York: Hastings House, 1975.

Missingham, Hal. **Close Focus.** Sydney Australia: Doubleday.

Pearson, John. **The Sun's Birthday.** New York: Doubleday & Co. Inc., 1973.

Porter, Eliot. **In Wildness is the Preservation of the World.** New York: Ballantine Books, Inc. 1976.

______.**Galapagos, Vol. 2** New York: Ballantine Books, Inc., 1970.

______. **The Place No One Knew.** New York: Ballantine Books, Inc.

Strache, Wolfe, **Forms and Patterns in Nature.** New York: Pantheon Books, 1973.

Time-Life Library of Photography. **Photographing Nature.** New York: Time-Life Books, 1971.

Victoria & Albert Museum catalog. **The Land.** 1976.

Weston, Brett. **Brett Weston-Voyage of the Eye.** Millerton, New York: Aperture, Inc., 1975.

Design source photographs by Irene Waller.
Photographs of completed works, unless otherwise credited, by Irene and Geoffrey Waller.